Thank you for coming so

far to be with us

Bill Bane

August '05

Wm. F. Bane

We Did It Their Way

Edited by
Mary Kay Matson and Oka Negley

ISBN 0-9652452-0-9

Library of Congress Catalog Card Number: 96-076761

Dedication

To my wonderful wife and our two great sons: a book could be written about each of them.

Elizabeth took a job for $1 an hour after our youngest son, Donnie, started school. She walked three miles a day in all kinds of weather for that modest pay and it helped during a hard financial time in our lives.

Our sons worked from the time they were old enough to do chores around the house and continued to work all through school. Billy, our first son, started our business and, in the early years, often worked seven days a week.

Lois (Billy's wife) and Linda Faye (Donnie's wife) are especially appreciated for their understanding and for the support they give their husbands.

Special Thanks

Special thanks are due to the customers of our service company in Indianapolis and the customers of our supply company, who are located in all parts of the world.

None of our success would have been possible without their trust and loyalty.

Acknowledgments

Many people contributed to this book in many different ways. The superb men and women who make up our company are the best at what they do, and their contributions are gratefully acknowledged. Vendors also have had a prominent place in the growth and success of our company.

The mists of memory and time will no doubt cause some to be missed, but following are listed many of those who have had a role in the development of our company and who are not mentioned in the text of this book.

George Abell	Ron Bouchard	John DeSantis
Ron Akers	Angelina Boulos	Dwain Dickerson
Mary Allison	Nora Bowling	Ethel Dillinger
Randall Amos	Lolita Brady	Dave Disser
Andy Anderson	Mike Bright	Jim Douglas
Bettye and Watt	Larry Brown	Beverly Downey
Anderson	Phil Brown	Andy Edwards
B. J. Anderson	Alan Bryson	Jeff Eicher
Bob Armstrong	Tom Buschmann	Kelly Eldridge
Kent Arvin	Michelle Bush	Quentin Eller
Mike Atkins	Jack Buckhorn	Brad Eubank
Michael Bagley	Dan Cahill	Paul Ferguson
Leslie Baker	Harry Cangany	Ray Fichter
Richard Baker	Vickie Chenowith	Mike Fitzgerald
Pete Baldwin	Jim Clark	Bill Franzmann
Gene Barbour	John Coons	Bill Gammons
David Barrett	Brent Cooper	Jeff Germain
Barry Bauman	Bill Cordell	Dr. Robert E. Godfrey
Barney Bazin	Richard Corkhill	Herbert Gordon
Stella Benefiel	Earl Cornelieus	Marian Grate
George Bennett	Leon Cosby	Mary Green
Jim Bennett	Bob Croak	Al Greer
Sue Biemer	Bob Darmer	John Guthrie
Herb Binkley	Lea Davis	Dale Habel
Harry Black	Tommi Davis	Joe Halas
Velma Blume	John DeCosta	John Hammond
Steve Bohnert	Sean DeCosta	Dottie Hanna
Paul Bosler	Jim Deel	George Hartell

Drew Heimer
Bill Henderson
Jerry Hilardes
Jerry Hinchmann
Larry Hinds
Andy Holland
Kelly Hone
Bill House
Neal Howe
Greg Imel
Leonard Jackman
Joe James
Al Jancek
Scott Jenkins
Tricia Jenkins
Jeff Johnson
Linda Johnston
George Jones
Paul Jones
Linda Kanouse
Deena Keasey
Rick Kehl
Betty Kennard
John Kerrigan
Roger Kiley
Bob Kirby
Jeff Kiser
Sally Kjeldsen
Rick Klein
Rick Knight
Joe Knue
Dick and Eileen
    Koss
Karl Krause
George Lamb
James Lawrence
Carl Leimgruber
Bill Lindsay
Henry Lindsay
Fred Livingston
Larry Logan
Gloria Lombardo
Vince Lombardo
Bruce Longbottom
Richard Magnuson
Bill Mason
Bill Matheny

Sharon McAllister
Gloria McCollough
Dottie McGoff
Doug McQueen
Harry Meyers
Margaret Middleton
Doug Miley
Harry Miller
Jeff Miller
Kimberly Moore
Sue Moore
Ed Moss
Jack Moss
Peter Moss
Pat Moran
Mike Morris
Tom Morris
Harry Nahmias
James Nolden
Mike Noone
Doug Norris
Chirley Nye
Jim O'Connor
Jim Oliger
Soo Park
Ron Patterson
Mary Ann Petruzzi
Fred Phinisee
Jeff Polley
John Purcell
Bill Qualls
Jim Quick
Bob Quillen
Mike Richardson
Jim Roberts
Andrew Rogers
David Ross
Ken Rubush
Mike Russell
Phil Russo
John Sabin
Paul Sanders
Mike Schaefer
Steve Schaefer
Hank Schildmeier
Bob Schubert
Karl Schubert

Dick Schulz
Tom Schulz
Steve Schuster
Phil Searcy
Frank Shelton
Glen Shilling
Bill Sichting
Ginnie Simms
Catherine Simpson
Tom Shinn
Jeff Slipher
Brian Smith
Rod Snell
Janet Stackhouse
Bill Stark
Elbert Staten
Mary Stiles
Craig Stonebraker
Mike Stonebraker
J. D. Stratton
Catherine Szakel
Don Taylor
John Tirmerstein
Sandra Tripp
Dale Turpin
Bob Tzucker
Laura Van Dyke
Mark Van Westrum
Earl Washington
Mike Wells
Gordon Wheatley
Jim Whelan
Fred Whitley
Mike Williams
Del Willoughby
Todd Worl
Brent Wright
Odell Wright
Scott Wright
Todd Wright
Walt Wright
John Yeadon
Mike Yeadon
Wendi Young
Brad Zeigler
Terry Zimpleman
Jeff Zollner

Table of Contents

The story in this book parallels that of Horatio Alger. My family literally went from rags to riches, proving that the time-worn cliches about hard work, perseverance and determination are all true. All of the good things that have happened to us were the result of doing it their (the customer's) way.

The proof of our success is in the files of our service company in Central Indiana which contain more than 45,000 current customers. In our other business, we supply thousands of customers throughout the world who are in the cleaning business. Customers do not stay loyal to someone who does not do it their way.

In my career I have seen the cleaning business literally explode from a ragtag, fly-by-night state to the multi-billion dollar industry it is today. I have witnessed the evolution of the tools of the trade along with the maturing and development of the people in the business.

For years people have encouraged me to write a book. Some suggested that it be my life story. Most said it should be about the cleaning industry. Others have maintained it should deal with my "secrets of success."

First and foremost, my life has not been spectacular in the sense of fame or notoriety. I lead a conservative life style which would make very dull reading. Rather than a laborious effort to enshrine my own accomplishments, I will recall some of the most significant influences on my life and how they affected the success of our company.

Many of the reflections in this book will deal with the maturing of the carpet cleaning industry as I have seen it develop since I became a part of it in 1962.

I

The Groundwork for Success

Support and Inspiration

It has been said that behind every successful man there is a great woman. There have been two great women in my life. My maternal grandparents raised me from the age of two.

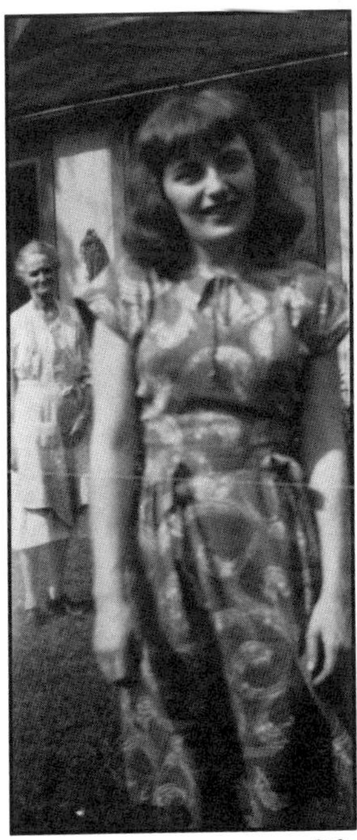

The two women in my life at their first meeting.

Frances Helen Bouquet Ryle, my grandmother, was a saintly woman, devout in her religious beliefs. She instilled values in me that have guided me through life.

"Mamaw" lived to see me marry Elizabeth Ann Woods, who would become my lifetime partner, mother of our children and my inspiration. Always supportive, always positive, Elizabeth gave me the luxury of knowing that anything I did was going to receive her full cooperation.

The influence of these two women and the support, effort and hard work of my two loyal sons, Bill, Jr., and Don, are without a doubt the overwhelming reasons for our success. On the following pages,

I will call them Billy and Donnie since that is the way I address them in real life.

One fact should be evident all through this book. A family that works together is unbeatable.

The Great Depression

I was born in the fourteen-room Victorian house that had been built by my great-grandparents in Indianapolis. My experience and background have their roots in being raised during the Great Depression. I was educated at Holy Cross Grade School by the Sisters of Providence from Terre Haute, Indiana, and at Cathedral High School by the Brothers of the Holy Cross from Notre Dame.

During the 1930s, life for many people was hard . . . even cruel. My grandfather, Irvin Matson Ryle, worked for Kingan & Co., a meat packing firm. At the very darkest part of the depression, Gramp worked twelve-hour days, six-day weeks, and earned twelve dollars each payday. He and Mamaw often would discuss how blessed we were that he had such a good job. He was a big, strong man

Gramp and me in 1933.

and disciplined me when I needed it as I was growing up.

He walked to work to save the streetcar fare, which was only seven cents. We were poor by today's standards. There was no telephone, automobile or other luxury that we consider a necessity now. We didn't have a radio or indoor plumbing until 1934. In spite of these inconveniences, we lived pretty well and considered ourselves better off than many of our neighbors.

We were never hungry or without clothing. Mamaw fed hundreds of people who were without work or food during those desperate years. We lived about six blocks from the railroad tracks and hoboes would find their way to our back door regularly. I believe they must have had a mark on our back fence to identify an easy handout. But, as bad as things were during the darkest part of the depression, we never locked our doors, which was a luxury by today's standards. Hungry and destitute as people were in those days, they did not break into homes. They asked for work and food, and those who could, shared with them.

Going to church was our entire social life. We were appreciative for what we had and were very happy. The Great Depression was a time in which prudence, perseverance, faith and frugality were a matter of everyday life and the experience surely helped form my conservative beliefs.

United States Marine Corps

When I was in high school I had two friends who wanted to join the Marines. Every time we were together, Vic Deering and Denny Wolbert would say, "Let's join the Marines. The war's going to be over before we get in if we don't do it soon."

They were both a little older than I was, and on my seventeenth birthday, June 25, 1944, the "three musketeers,"

CHAPTER ONE

as we were known, went downtown to enlist. The recruiting station was on the second floor above Kresge's Five and Dime. There was a long flight of steps up a narrow hallway, and we bounded to the top as though we were charging up a hill in combat.

After a short wait, we were ushered into private interview rooms where a noncommissioned officer talked about the Marine Corps. When I finished with the interview, he ushered me into another office. A captain, the officer in charge, gave me a form which would need to be signed by my grandparents, who were my legal guardians.

When I came out of his office, Vic and Denny were nowhere in sight. The sergeant on the desk told me they had gone. Both the captain and the sergeant seemed very nice and gave me the impression that this was going to be a great experience. I went home, got the form signed, delivered it to the captain and was sworn in. That evening I saw Vic and Denny at the drug store, and they told me they had changed their minds and had not enlisted.

When I came home on my boot camp leave, I told Denny and Vic how great it was at Parris Island: how new recruits were met at the train, served a wonderful meal before being tucked in for the night, and about the beautiful girls who were waiting at the gate every night for us to get off duty. Denny enlisted right away, and the next time we saw one another he had a few choice words for me about the reality of his experiences in boot camp.

Vic never fell for my story.

Semper Fi!

The reality of the Marine Corps was that an old gunnery sergeant named Lou Diamond met us as we got off cattle trucks at the entrance to the narrow causeway that led to Parris Island. He personally kicked every man in the slats as a greeting. We were assigned to Platoon 131, had our heads shaved, got a sparse clothing issue and a meal at the mess hall of cold hot dogs and baked beans. After chow, we were issued a bucket and brush and given a quonset hut to scrub. About midnight, we drew a mattress, sheets and a blanket from the quartermaster's shack. We finally got to sleep about 1:30 a.m. What a day!

The next thing I remember was a big, mean drill instructor banging me on the bottom of my feet with his swagger stick at 4:30 in the morning. It got worse from there. There was no liberty; there were no movies except training films; no girls; no days off; and nothing but discipline and hard work for three solid months. The story I told Denny Wolbert was a little different.

Command

I served under many commanders during my five years in the Corps. All of them influenced the way I deal with people. But, two of these officers come to mind as having the most impact on my attitude. Both were colonels at the time I knew them.

In early 1945, in advanced combat training at Camp LeJeune, North Carolina, I served under Colonel Lewis B. "Chesty" Puller. The colonel would order a twenty-five mile forced march under full field pack, head up the column himself, and walk with his men the entire way. He carried his own pack, too. Chesty Puller was literally everywhere, overseeing all phases of our combat training. He was a highly-decorated combat veteran and seemed driven to teach us how to survive.

Colonel T. W. P. Murphy was in charge of a motor transport company to which I was attached in 1946. On difficult convoys the Colonel traveled in his comfortable bus, with enlisted personnel assigned to walk Susie, his German Shepherd dog, shine his boots and do other chores the Colonel found necessary when he was "roughing it."

Colonel Puller's troops would follow him into hell. Colonel Murphy, on the other hand, was not held in high esteem by his Marines. It's not hard to imagine which of these two commanders I admired.

The Big Bombs

When the atomic bombs were dropped on Hiroshima and Nagasaki in Japan, our unit was attached to the Fourth Marine Division, which had been devastated in the battle for Iwo Jima. Training was geared to the invasion of the Island Empire of Japan.

The island-hopping battles for Iwo Jima, Saipan and Okinawa had shown that the Japanese were fanatical in their belief of death before surrender. There was every reason to believe this fanaticism would increase when their homeland was under siege.

Just a few weeks after "Little Boy" was dropped from the Enola Gay, our training command was broken up, and seven of us from the battalion were transferred to a motor transport company and shipped to Philadelphia.

W. C. Fields was said to have despised Philadelphia and supposedly requested his epitaph to read, "All things considered, I'd rather be here than in Philadelphia."

I would rather be in Philadelphia anytime. Had that terrible bomb not been dropped, the war would have continued and many thousands of us would have become casualties. By not being transferred to Philly, I wouldn't have met Elizabeth, and you wouldn't be reading this book about the cleaning business.

Elizabeth, after Easter Mass, with our 1935 DeSoto.

April 26, 1947, was a happy day.

Tanker Driver

After my four-year hitch ended in 1948, I drove a gasoline transport for Gaseteria, a family-owned and operated business in Indianapolis, Indiana. I learned to drive tractor-trailer units in the Corps, so it was easy to get a job as a truck driver when I got out. Even though I only spent two years there, the management techniques of Gaseteria were admired, absorbed and retained.

One of the advertising slogans of the company was, "You never have to honk for service." The men who worked in Gaseteria service stations would actually run out to an automobile and be there by the time the wheels stopped turning. Service was the main topic of conversation, and the station managers were almost fanatical about taking care of customers. That attitude was reflected throughout the ranks. The customer service instinct was instilled in me by that company.

Employees were called by their first names, which seemed strange after four years in the military, but that was the style of Russell Williams and his two sons, who were the principals of the company. Employees were treated with respect and their opinions were solicited on a regular basis. The men and women of the company were enthusiastic and optimistic about the future of the organization.

Mr. Russell, as he was affectionately known throughout the company, died in an airplane crash and Gaseteria was subsequently purchased by a major oil company.

Armored Cars

The Korean War erupted on June 25, 1950. I don't have trouble remembering the date because it was my birthday and I was recalled to active duty in the Marine Corps. I was discharged in 1951 and took a job with Brink's, Inc., an armored car service. Guns and trucks were all that I knew, so this seemed like a logical choice for employment.

Founded in 1859, this company was not at all like Gaseteria in its philosophy. A cold, corporate hand reached from the main office in Chicago to its many branches. Employees belonged to the Teamsters' Union and there was an antagonistic relationship between Union members and management.

People who did their jobs efficiently were frowned upon by those who dragged their feet in the quest for overtime. I didn't like the way the company was managed, but I always had a deep-down resentment for those who goofed off.

Brink's was managed in an overly frugal manner that often resulted in trucks breaking down because of skimpy maintenance. One day in 1953, I was in charge of a route called the "city run." Our four-man crew was responsible for handling bank transfers, government shipments, department store receipts and deposits for many different businesses in the downtown area.

In mid-morning our truck broke down. Because of other trucks being deadlined for repairs, there was no spare truck. T. T. Wilson, the branch manager, called a car rental agency, and we finished the day's activities in a Ford station wagon. Everyone on my crew was extremely nervous without the protection of the armored vehicle. There was no safe in the station wagon and no armored plating or bulletproof glass. We handled millions of dollars that day and our only protection was an old Winchester rifle and our .38 caliber service revolvers.

Bill Sieg and I both hired on in July of 1951. He was about ready to retire in 1980 when he was ambushed, shot and killed while carrying the day's receipts from a Kmart store to his truck. Elizabeth has said many times that it could have been me. Every time I see an armored car on the street, I thank God that I'm not on board. Ironically, that Kmart was just two blocks north of the building that houses our business on north Keystone Avenue.

Baseball

Baseball has always been a love of my life. I played the game as a youngster and managed teams for eighteen years in Little League, Pony League, Connie Mack and American Legion Baseball. These youth programs were, without a doubt, one of the greatest joys of my life. They represented entertainment, release and a sense of accomplishment.

While I never had the athletic skill of my two sons or many of the young men who played for me over the years, I found that I did have an ability to communicate and teach the fundamentals of the game. In fact, I found that it is easier to tell people what to do than it is to do it yourself, especially if they can do it better than you.

As a baseball manager, my teams won city, state and regional championships. The game teaches teamwork, especially for managers. Playing the strengths and weaknesses of the various individuals in the right position makes a winner. Managing a baseball team also makes one look ahead two or three innings. Planning and strategy become instinctive. All of these elements have a strong correlation in business.

Billy in Little League

Learning Experiences

These experiences taught me: discipline, in the Marine Corps; how employees like to be treated, at Gaseteria; how not to treat employees, at Brink's; and how to develop teamwork and think ahead, in baseball. Each has had a profound effect on my management philosophies.

Five years in the Marines, two years driving a gasoline transport and thirteen years in the armored car business shaped my management skills and work habits. Being a father taught me other lessons which would prove to be invaluable in my business career.

1962 Little League City Champs. Donnie is third from left in front row. I'm at the left rear.

1963 Pony League Champs. Donnie is second from left in front row. I'm at the left rear.

1969 State Championship Team. Ron Baker and Donnie are in the top row on the left. Marc Jones is seated behind the bat boy holding the trophy. I'm No. 4.

1971 State Champions. I'm on the far right.

II

Our Own Business

How It All Began

Our cleaning service was not intended to be a permanent business. My oldest son, Billy, wanted to attend an expensive new preparatory school, and quite frankly, we just couldn't afford it. Elizabeth worked as an assistant for Dr. James P. Leeds, an optometrist, and Billy asked if he could clean the office every Sunday. This provided a part-time business for Billy and paid part of the tuition he needed for the school.

Billy started the business with a capital investment of twenty dollars. I have a folder in my office with his first notes about the money he put in and his expenditures. Billy always was very dependable and worked hard at anything he did. He is highly competitive and does not do anything in which he cannot excel.

We knew he would do a good job for Dr. Leeds. The concern for detail he developed on this job would help make him a great manager later in his career. Our youngest son, Donnie, was

Billy and Donnie
June, 1961

23

just eleven the day our company was founded. That Sunday morning, February 4, 1962, we all went with Billy to help him clean Dr. Leeds' office. Donnie worked right along with us. We earned the princely sum of ten dollars.

Donnie had a paper route and got up at 4:00 a.m. to deliver *The Indianapolis Star*. He was always very thrifty, worked hard, and saved the money he earned. These attributes would prepare him to become treasurer of our company one day.

When Donnie was nine years old, he organized the "Worthy Cause Bank." He put in his own savings and sold shares to the rest of us to raise capital. Loans were made, mostly to his mother, but I remember one time when Billy wanted to take out a loan and there was no money in the bank. All of it had been loaned out, and Billy demanded to redeem his shares. The crisis passed, thankfully, and since that day we have had no major disagreements about the management of the family's finances.

One of Donnie's favorite expressions in those early years in business was that "we live together, pray together, work together and play together." I think sometimes he said this in anguish.

Full-Time Business

Dr. Leeds was in an association with two other doctors who had offices at different locations. Before long we were cleaning all three offices. Referrals to other professional offices brought in additional business, and before we knew it, we had a full-fledged office-cleaning firm in operation. Several of my co-workers at Brink's worked part time for us. In December, 1964, I left Brink's and became a full-time employee of our service company.

The decision to leave my full-time job was not an easy one, but after nearly two years of working in the business part time, the family decided it was the right thing to do. I gave Brink's notice on December 15, 1964, that I would be leaving on January 15, 1965. I was fired the next day. Apparently, it was decided that I would become eligible for three weeks' vacation at the beginning of the new year, and this prompted the dismissal. As I left his office, Ed Talley, who was the manager of the Indianapolis branch, said, "Merry Christmas, Bill!"

During the next two years the business grew to thirty-seven employees, with accounts such as professional offices, truck terminals, a meat packing firm, and the regional air route traffic control center at the airport.

Family Council

When we incorporated the business in 1966, against the advice of our accountant and lawyer, we issued the shares of the company in increments of 25 percent to each member of the family. Counsel advised that one individual should have a controlling interest, but we decided that everyone was equally responsible for the success or failure of the company, so everyone should share equally in the ownership. The corporation has survived and prospered even though we did not follow professional advice.

When our boys were very young, we held family councils to discuss plans or problems. The four of us would vote on an issue. If the vote was tied, we would put the various decisions on pieces of paper and Tabby, our old cat, would pick one.

Our corporation is not run exactly like that, but we have regular meetings with the four principal shareholders, and every

Tabby

month the officers and managers of the corporation meet to discuss strategies. Management is by consensus, since we no longer have Tabby to break the tie votes.

Troubles with Carpet Cleaning

Some of our office cleaning contracts called for the carpets to be cleaned once or twice a year. This seemingly simple chore gave us more trouble than any other single phase of the maintenance business. The search for answers to carpet cleaning problems was ongoing and solutions were evasive, but it led to the development of our own unique method.

In 1963, I saw an ad in *Popular Mechanics* magazine that made carpet cleaning sound easy, so we sent $745 to the manufacturers in Racine, Wisconsin. A machine and some supplies arrived in a box, and we had to figure out assembly and how to use it. I was so proud of it. I told Claude, my barber, about the new machine, and he had me come over to his house and clean a bedroom with white carpeting. The next day, there were streaks of brown all over the room, and we thought the floor finish had come through the carpet. No one knew about "browning" in those days, much less how to cure the problem. I bought new carpet for Claude's bedroom.

The machine didn't work very well, but it was a start in the business that would become our life's work, so I have always had a warm spot in my heart for Francis U. Von Schrader, the manufacturer of the machine.

During the next few years we used rotary scrubbers, dry foam, and powder products. With all of them, resoiling would occur at a rapid rate. On many occasions building managers would point out that we had just "cleaned" their carpets and already spots were reappearing. Discoloration and matting were the rule rather than the exception. Discouraged as we were, we stayed with it because more and more of the hard surface floors we maintained were being covered with carpeting.

Here Comes Steam

In the late 1960s the steam extraction method was introduced to the carpet cleaning industry. The machines were heavy, inefficient, and not widely accepted by the cleaning community. Deep Steam Extraction and Steamway were two of the early pioneers in modern steam cleaning. The machines used by both companies were portable and employed heavy drag-back floor tools. Steamatic was the first franchise in the industry and had a machine that was very similar to Deep Steam's. We looked at all of them.

A salesman demonstrated a Steamtronic carpet cleaner for us in 1968. The cleaning head weighed about eighty-five pounds and there were only fifteen feet of hoses, so the tanks and base unit had to be carried around the job, too. They must have weighed three hundred and fifty pounds. The equipment had obnoxious little rollers that made it difficult to move over the carpet and nearly impossible to negotiate up and down stairs.

The carpet stayed wet for more than a day following the demonstration. There was a discoloration on the tips of the carpet fibers when they finally dried, and the carpet felt crusty. But, in spite of those negative developments, we were convinced of the many benefits of extraction cleaning and began thinking of ways to improve the process and make it practical, economical and efficient to use in our business.

Twenty Acres of Carpet

Later that same year, I got even more excited about carpet cleaning when Indiana National Bank announced that their new building would contain twenty acres of carpeting. Ironically, it would be fifteen years before we would clean in that building. Eventually we contracted all forty Indiana National Bank branches throughout the city.

Another thing that excited us about the carpet cleaning business was how much we could charge for shampooing carpets. For example, in 1967 we maintained hard surface floors in a Porky Lane supermarket. It took five men, an automatic scrubber, two rotary machines, assorted chemicals, stripper, sealer and floor finish to complete a job for which we charged five cents a square foot.

By contrast, one rotary scrubber with a shampoo tank attached, a wet vac, a jug of shampoo, and two men could charge

Twenty acres of carpet in that building!

ten cents a square foot for working on carpet. It didn't take a genius to like that difference.

Residential Carpet Cleaning

We were tired of the maintenance business. It was not very profitable and we worked nights, Sundays and holidays. It was a twenty-four hour per day, three hundred sixty-five day per year business. Mostly bid work, the low bidder usually got the job.

Besides not being able to pay our people what they were worth, our clients had a habit of making us wait for our money. Ninety days to collect an account was the rule rather than the exception. We worked for Kmart and would be locked in a store at closing time and let out at 7:00 in the morning. In addition to the mistrust they showed toward maintenance people, they were very slow payers. Our help was always paid more than the going rate, and with the slow-pay nature of our accounts receivable, we just couldn't make a decent profit.

A residential carpet cleaning operation, we believed, would be a quick cash-turn business. It would be a daytime operation, and we would accept payment by cash, check or charge card, any of which would be in our bank account that night or next day, at the latest.

What a joy that it worked out that way!

Commercial Carpet Cleaning

We knew that a certain amount of commercial work would be required for our new carpet cleaning company, especially in the winter when the residential market would slow down in our snowy climate. We decided to concentrate on the residential market, anyway.

Our theory was that as we gained longevity in the residential sector, we would be invited to "quote," not "bid," on offices and industrial properties. We knew that all of the owners and managers of businesses lived someplace, and if we cleaned their homes and did a good job, we would be invited to clean where they worked. By being invited, we could charge more than if we were required to bid the job. This theory proved to be absolutely correct.

Since 1969, we have left bid work for the competition.

Not Proud of Our Work !

We did not get into residential carpet cleaning earlier because I was very uncomfortable with the methods we were using. In 1965, I used a J. I. Holcomb rotary machine and Holcomb shampoo to clean the living room carpet for Sally and Jim Revelli, who were friends and neighbors. There was an extremely dirty area in front of their fireplace so I really poured the shampoo to it.

The next morning Sally called and asked me to come over. There was a slight problem. The carpet had been so wet that, when it shrank, it had such force it pulled a floor board up in front of the fireplace. I had to repair the floor before I stretched the carpet back.

Not long after that experience, I declined a request from Oka Negley to clean the carpets in her home. Oka and her husband Pete were friends, and I had to confess that I didn't want to foam, soak or powder their carpets. In 1976, Oka joined our firm and today serves as my Administrative Assistant. Had I cleaned her carpets ten years earlier, we may have ceased to be friends, which would have been a terrible loss for our company, since Oka has become a key person in the management of our many business interests.

III

Inventing A Cleaning System

The Basic Design

Our plan to build truck-mounted, extraction-type carpet cleaning equipment was devised in early 1969. Using available technology and with the help of an air-movement engineer, we began to develop an idea that would leave all of the heavy equipment on the truck. The truck-mounted concept came from my experience with Gaseteria. They had a fleet of fuel oil delivery trucks which had long hoses, mounted on electric reels. They could quickly and efficiently deliver fuel oil to hard-to-reach locations.

The 1949 Dodge fuel oil truck that inspired the truck-mounted concept for our carpet cleaning business twenty years later.

A power take-off unit from the truck engine drove the pumps. That was my first thought for powering the cleaning equipment. But, in exploring the idea with automotive people, I found that a light truck engine, such as we would be using, would not hold up well with prolonged running at a fast idle. An automotive engineer told me he feared that piston slap would develop and that valves would form carbon deposits quickly because of the back-pressure created by operating the engine without a full load.

A small gasoline engine was our next choice for powering the cleaning pumps. However, maintenance problems, questionable dependability and operational costs made us look elsewhere.

Working from the truck rather than unloading equipment still made sense. We wanted to use one hundred fifty feet of hose so we could reach nearly any residential location. To work at that distance, a positive displacement vacuum pump, rather than the commonly used centrifugal vacuum motor, would be necessary. It would take a large vacuum pump to provide enough air velocity to move the water and soil through the static resistance of that much hose.

Anticipated problems in developing the necessary power to run the big pump were overcome, at least on paper. The answer was so obvious we almost overlooked it. An electric motor with a long extension cord plugged into a normal receptacle was the simple answer. With that hookup we could use cheap, dependable electricity for power.

An electrical engineer worked out a design that would allow us to run a large, powerful 1-1/2 horsepower motor and drive two pumps on only 12 amperes. This power source was readily available, dependable, and very economical. In fact, it would not cost us a cent to operate. I really liked this idea.

Considering what happened to the price of gasoline in the next few years, the development of electric power was, without a doubt, the factor which would separate us from all of our competition in the years ahead.

Built-In Quality

We had bought so much junk equipment that we were determined to build something that would last. All of the machines from various manufacturers that we had used were quickly obsolete. In fact, some of them were obsolete before we had paid for them. Stainless steel, brass and aluminum were specified for our new equipment so that longevity would be assured. There would be no cheap metals, plastic or built-in obsolescence in our machine.

The plans all looked good, but we had to have some money to build the prototype. We wanted to introduce this revolutionary new idea to the Indianapolis area with a marketing and promotional program. To fully equip two vehicles (one for each son), set up a new office, pay off existing obligations, and advertise and promote the business, we figured we would need about $50,000.

My Friendly Banker

I went to the Indiana National Bank, where I had done business for twenty years. I had visions of getting the $50,000 loan and a contract to clean the twenty acres of carpet in their new building. Armed with drawings of the equipment and a *pro forma* statement prepared by our CPA, Phil Eicher, I made a presentation to a vice-president of the bank. I thought it was pretty good.

When I finished, Fred Brenner sat back in his chair, thought for a moment, and then said, "Bill, I'm not going to give you $50,000, but I will give you some free advice. Why don't you give up this cockamamie idea with all the tanks, reels and hoses and go out and get a real job as a salesman? You did such a nice job on this presentation, you should be a salesman."

I was crushed. I went down the street to the American Fletcher National Bank and asked to see the manager, whose name was Lester Smith. I had known Mr. Smith from my years at Brink's. After telling him that Fred wouldn't lend me any money, I made the same presentation and this time did a little better.

I got $10,000 on the condition that I would move our business account to his bank. I agreed. The bank was having a promotion to sign up new accounts, and Mr. Smith gave me a rose bush that afternoon, which I planted behind our house. We called it our "money bush." It is still alive and well.

The Big Stock Sale

Phil Eicher came up with an idea to sell preferred stock to raise the rest of the $50,000. The plan called for selling the stock in increments of $5,000. The stock was offered to everyone I knew and even to some people I didn't know.

Marvin "Mac" Maguire was the manager of a company for whom we worked in the office cleaning business. Mac was first to sign up for the new stock issue and gave me his check for $5,000. It seemed so easy I just knew this was a great idea. Mac was also the last to sign on. When someone is asked for $5,000, it is astonishing to see the alacrity with which they

Phil Eicher, CPA, talks with Bane-Clene equipment owner about accounting at 1982 convention. Phil joined Bane-Clene in 1966.

suddenly discover a prior appointment or remember that all of their available funds are invested elsewhere.

After our stock drive fizzled, I called Mac to say the offering didn't sell. Since his was the only block of stock sold, the issue wouldn't be consummated. He said, "That's OK, Bill. Just consider it a loan." When I paid him back the next year, with interest, Mac commented, "I really never expected to see that money again."

Mac was a true friend.

Our Rolling Stock

The first two truck-mounts were built without the benefit of extra storage tanks or a portable base power unit. We

Old Number One—The '69 Dodge Van

bought a new 1969 Dodge van and a used 1968 Dodge that had about 20,000 miles on the odometer. This was before it was illegal for dealers to roll back the mileage. That used truck must have had 120,000 miles on it because we had to put a new engine in it during the first year.

Our fleet included a 1962 Rambler station wagon and a 1957 Chevrolet panel truck which we had used for a supply truck in the office cleaning business. We sold the station wagon to help with our capital shortage. A few years later, the '68 Dodge was sold to Larry Sparks, an employee who wanted to go into the business on his own. We still own the '69 Dodge van. The venerable old unit is on display in our showroom in Indianapolis with the original cleaning plant mounted inside.

Give Me $15,000 Worth

The loan proceeds from the bank and Mac's money were used for office equipment, two trucks and enough components to build two truck-mounted carpet cleaning units. The

Our first office

balance of the money was used to pay off obligations remaining from the maintenance business.

We set up shop in our home, which is what most folks in our business do. A used typewriter, small desk, single-line telephone and file cabinet outfitted our office. There were no funds left for an advertising program or the other equipment that is important to a new business. These had to be put off to a later time.

North Side Welding Company made the sixty gallon stainless steel tanks and frames for the truck units, and most of the assembly was done by us in our back yard. The first hose reels were old wooden cable reels that came from the Western Electric plant. In subsequent years, we hired various metal fabricators to do the heavy steel work.

Getting Started

Elizabeth left her full-time job and became our first telephone specialist. She had been making a good salary, and we really missed it during that first few months. Donnie was worried that she gave up her job, but I knew answering the calls properly would be the most important part of our new business. Having surveyed the competition, I found that most companies answered their phones with a recording. I just knew that Elizabeth would be our strongest asset in acquiring customers.

Move the Business Back Home Where It Started

Since Elizabeth did not drive, we made the decision to close our office on Tenth Street and operate out of our home. In

Our home when we bought it in 1952.

some ways, this seemed like a regression, but we felt it was extremely important for her to answer all incoming calls. We all agreed that operating from our home would save money.

We gave all of our janitorial contracts to employees and sold them the equipment that was on the job. We wanted out of the business so we could devote our full effort to carpet cleaning.

The Construction Business

The 1957 addition to our home.

It was apparent that we had to add a room to our home so we would have enough space to live and to work. To save money, Billy, Donnie and I did most of the construction ourselves. We excavated next to the house, added a basement room for our office, broke through to the existing basement for access and made steps down to the new office from the outside so people would not have to come through the house to access the business.

Dad and Billy do the work while Donnie clowns.

We left the upper floor unfinished for a year until the new business began to make money.

Marketing Plan

So, now we had two truck-mounts, two sons ready to work, a wife to answer the phone and make the appointments and me to call on prospective customers. The world seemed good. There was this one small problem: the lack of customers. Except for a few commercial accounts we had retained from the maintenance business, we didn't have enough work to keep one truck busy, much less two.

There were no funds for advertising and we were not in the Yellow Pages yet. Instead of letting us mope around the office, Elizabeth sent Billy and Donnie out to drive the two vans through the downtown area so people would see them. She sent me out knocking on doors at businesses and churches looking for work. It wasn't the greatest marketing plan, but it worked. I would meet friends who would say, "This new business of yours must be going great. I see your trucks all over town."

Starting the new addition to our home.

Enough Phones To Be A Bookie

The next year, we completed the room addition above ground and took over the rest of the basement for the growing business. Phone calls were increasing to the point that Indiana Bell Telephone Company installed a one-hundred-pair cable for phone service. The installers told me that the only residence they had ever seen with that many phone wires was the home of a bookie.

We even had a twenty-button telephone set installed in our bedroom. Elizabeth didn't want to miss a call and would answer the phone twenty-four hours a day. Most of the answers she developed to the many questions about our process are still used today. In fact, the forms she devised and the telephone procedures she initiated are used by thousands of successful businesses throughout the world. We never dreamed anything like this would be possible while we were digging that hole alongside our home for our new office.

Expansion

By the end of the second year, we had telephone stalls in every corner of the basement and points in between. The first few years were both exciting and frightening as business growth forced us to rent warehouse space for truck and chemical storage. The installation of equipment was now a part of our business, and we had freight trucks coming and going.

When we had moved to our home on Millersville Road, there were cows grazing on the land around our home. It was out in the country, but by the mid-sixties the city had caught up with us. Zoning was not a problem when we started our business, but it became something with which we had to deal as our business grew.

In 1972, we purchased the house next door as a buffer and use it today for record storage. By 1974 the business had consumed our entire home so we purchased the two properties directly across the street, and Elizabeth and I moved over there. The two homes were eventually joined together with an atrium that houses a swimming pool, and it has been a very comfortable

The old homestead has been expanded several times and today houses the corporate offices of Bane-Clene. Media Associates, a publishing and advertising subsidiary of Bane-Clene, is also head-quartered here.

place to live. It is a restful residence along a scenic waterway, and the fifteen acres provide a haven for us. We built a nature trail for exercise, and it is an easy walk to the office for me.

During the ensuing years, we purchased eight other properties adjacent to the place where our business began, and in effect, we became our own neighbors. Zoning was no longer a problem.

In May of 1978 we purchased commercial property on Keystone Avenue, which is less than two miles from our office/ home compound, and consolidated the equipment and supply business at that location. Two years later the telephone service operation was moved there from Millersville Road. The advertising agency and my offices remain at the old homestead.

Efforts Begin To Pay Off

One of our early marketing successes involved going to a church and offering to clean the whole place at no charge if a group would gather for a short demonstration. The size of the group would be determined by the square footage we would have to clean. Audiences ranged from twenty to sixty people. A small portion of the dirtiest area would be cleaned to show a dramatic contrast. A sample of the dirty water would be shown to the audience, and we would hand out literature. The entire demonstration took less than a half hour, and members were glad to donate this time to their church in order to have the carpets cleaned.

As soon as the crowd left, we finished cleaning all of the carpeted areas. An invoice in the amount of our normal cleaning charge was mailed to the church and marked "Complimentary." Sometimes as many as fifteen new customers would be generated out of these church demonstrations. In the year following the demonstration, more than half of those present would become customers.

The closest thing to real marketing we did that first year was to rent booth space at the Indiana State Fair. We put the new truck in the exhibit. We didn't miss it because there wasn't any work for it, anyway.

Elizabeth had an off-premises phone extension installed in our booth, and she ran the business from that location. A little one-color, single-fold flyer was all we had in the way of literature. With that humble effort, we began to build a customer base. The month after the State Fair, our Yellow Pages ad appeared for the first time, and business began to come our way.

During the next four years we exhibited at the State Fair, Gift and Hobby Show, Home Show, and Flower and Patio

Show. The opportunity to meet people and talk one-on-one was invaluable since it helped hone our skills in talking about our process.

This experience would become extremely valuable later when we began selling our equipment to other people in the carpet cleaning business.

Bill and Elizabeth at 1971
Flower and Patio Show in Indianapolis

IV

The Equipment Supply Business

Threat of A Lawsuit

The cleaning system we developed in 1969 was never intended to be sold to others in the business. The two truck-mounted units we built were for our own new service company. But, fate would dictate otherwise.

In early 1970, we cleaned carpets in the home of Morris Ouellette. He was apparently fascinated and impressed, because he called me a few days later to compliment me on my two sons and the job they had done. He went on to say that he had a son he would like to put in the cleaning business and asked where he could buy the equipment. I told him that we had built it ourselves and that it was not for sale. Besides, I wasn't interested in having a competitor use our system.

A few weeks later, Mr. Ouellette threatened us with a lawsuit for restraint of trade and several other charges. I didn't believe he could do this, but at this tender stage in our new business, the last thing we needed was a lawsuit. Fearing such legal action, we capitulated to his demands and built a truck-mounted carpet cleaning unit for him.

That event heralded our entry into the supply side of the cleaning industry. Morrie's son, Phillip, was a good competitor and never hurt our business at all. Besides, we made a little profit on the transaction. Since that time, we have supplied and trained many cleaning firms in our prime market area of Central Indiana.

Good competitors make more business for everyone by helping to stimulate the potential market.

Compliments, for a Change

The significance of our invention became obvious in a very short time. What really told us we had a winner was that our customers were impressed. Compliments are rare in the service business, and all of a sudden we were getting nice notes and complimentary telephone calls about our new service.

Inside a customer's home, there was just the whisper of air and the rushing sound of the spray. All of the heavy equipment was outside in the truck, along with the moist, muggy, foul air we exhausted through the vacuum hose. Our customers loved the work we were doing and told their friends and neighbors about our new service.

But the real enlightenment was yet to come.

The First Design

Our first equipment design did not have the capability of portable operation. High-rise and security work, where the doors had to be closed, presented a problem. So, the detachable base power unit was added in 1970. With this development, we discovered one of the major advantages to our new method of cleaning.

When we took the portable base unit into a work area in a high-rise building, the carpet took nearly twice as long to dry than on a residential job where we operated with the base unit outside in the truck. On commercial jobs, we found that by leaving the base unit outside the area being cleaned, the drying process was cut nearly in half because all the moist air was being exhausted away from the work area. Odors were exhausted instead of being allowed to permeate other furnishings and to re-enter the freshly cleaned carpet.

"External Extraction" Is Born

Now we knew we had the perfect system to sell to the rest of the industry. What we didn't realize was how difficult it would be to sell the truck-mounted concept. Phil Eicher, our CPA, adamantly opposed our going into the supply business. He suggested that we concentrate on our local cleaning operation. We did, and the business quickly turned the corner and was in the black. The loan from the bank and Mac's loan were repaid in less than two years.

In spite of this success, we were intrigued with the potential of the supply business and began mailing brochures to some cleaning businesses in Indiana. Later, we placed a small advertisement in a trade magazine. That was the beginning of our national marketing program for truck-mounted cleaning equipment.

We were the first in the industry to use the terms "truck-mounted" and "external extraction."

A Hard Market

Resistance to our new truck-mounted product and concept was unbelievable. Established cleaners didn't want to give up their investment in shampoo and dry foam equipment to take a chance on something new. Those who had bought portable steam cleaning equipment were, for the most part, disenchanted and didn't even want to talk about steam.

New people who were thinking about getting into the cleaning business were hesitant to invest several thousand dollars for equipment, when a few hundred dollars at the local janitorial supply house would get them started with shampoo machines.

I'll Throw in a Truck

In 1972, we wanted to trade in the old '57 Chevy panel truck on a new Ford Econoline van. The Ford dealer offered us fifty dollars, and I remember saying that I would rather give that old Chevy truck away than let him have it for fifty dollars.

At the time, I was negotiating to sell a truck-mounted unit to Gordon Cassell in Frankfort, Indiana. I said, "Gordy, I'll tell you what I'll do. You buy this machine and I'll throw in a truck." Gordy did, and he drove that old Chevy truck for about ten years.

The old Chevy truck

Sales Leads?

A business reply card was attached to our early equipment sales brochure, and it was not unusual to get names and phone numbers in response to our mailers. Calling these respondents was an experience in itself. A janitorial firm in Brazil, Indiana, returned the reply card without including a phone number. I called "Information" and was told the company had an unlisted telephone number. A business with an unlisted phone? That should have been a warning of things to come.

In the mid '70s, I began using trade magazines for advertising. A reader who wanted more information would return a postcard to the magazine listing his or her name, address, and phone number. I would try to call the prospect to set up an appointment. Many that I did reach by phone would deny they had sent in the card for information. Either they were lying or the trade magazine had sent us names of people who really hadn't inquired.

Some of those who responded were a treat. I remember driving all the way to Sea Girt, New Jersey, in 1975 to demonstrate our equipment. After I got there, the man asked me to clean a commercial job. When we got around to talking about closing the sale, he told me that he really didn't have any money to buy equipment, but that he really needed that job done.

Later that year, the same thing happened in Bowling Green, Kentucky. I did a demonstration for a janitorial service in a school. When I finished cleaning the cafeteria carpet, which had been loaded with shampoo and dry foam, I took the man to the Holiday Inn for dinner and to close the sale. The demonstration had been so dramatic that he would just have to buy our equipment. That is when he admitted to me that he really couldn't afford to buy equipment. He just needed to have that job done to save his contract. He even developed a tear in his eye for my benefit.

I had an appointment one day in 1972 with a man in South Bend, Indiana. After I finished the demonstration, he said he never intended to buy equipment. He just wanted to see how it worked. That same cold night, I drove through a blizzard to Logansport, Indiana. I got there a half hour ahead of my appointment time at 7:00 p.m. I waited until after midnight, but the man never did arrive. What a day!

Billy and I drove to Cincinnati, Ohio, one morning in a dangerous heavy fog. Our appointment was at 6:00 a.m. with a janitorial firm. They didn't show up. Another time we drove to Connersville, Indiana, a town about seventy miles from home. The temperature was 15° below zero. Our Dodge truck didn't have a very good heater, and we almost froze. When we got ready to demonstrate, our hoses were frozen.

That happened to be in the home of Don Barrett, Jr., who would later become a strong friend and supporter in the carpet industry. His father was a carpet retailer and Don says he doesn't remember the episode, since he was just a young lad and was probably at school.

Billy and I remember the day very well.

Real Hard Heads

One time we drove to Muncie, Indiana, to demonstrate for someone who had sent in one of those reply cards. When we were finished cleaning half of the man's living room, he told us to stop. Then he ceremoniously opened a pair of sliding doors to an adjoining dining room, much like theater curtains would be opened. There was a dry-foam machine all poised and ready to go to work. "Now I'm going to show you guys how to clean a carpet," he said pompously. It did our hearts good to see that he couldn't get his side of the room clean. He was still running his machine back and forth when we left.

Many large firms exercised us while they were trying to find out more about the new steam carpet cleaning method. In 1975, Walter Griese, a ServiceMaster operator from New Jersey, spent several days with us in Indianapolis. While he observed our operation on location, Mr. Griese offended one of our department store customers, which resulted in a call to their customer service department. He had a thousand questions that nearly drove our staff up the wall.

Kevin Stark

Kevin Stark, who at the time was a cleaning technician, was saddled with the responsibility of taking Mr. Griese out on the job. When Kevin would answer his questions, he would invariably say, "That's a good point, Kevin." Kevin paraphrases that today with a retort, "That's a good point, Walter," whenever someone explains something rather well.

Later that year, Mr. Griese asked me to drive to West Orange, New Jersey, to demonstrate our equipment for his partner. They never did buy anything from us, and I always suspected that he had an interest in a supply organization.

Experiences such as these sometimes made us want to quit.

Billy's Tie

Not all of our early demonstrations were quite so bad, and the few good ones we had kept us interested in the supply business. In 1974, Billy and I went to Bloomington, Indiana, to demonstrate our cleaning machine at Indiana University. We met a contingent of representatives which included purchasing, maintenance and administrative people. There were eight in all and they were as stodgy a group as I had ever seen to that point.

Midway through our demonstration, Billy bent over the open tank of the machine and his tie dipped into the water. Without missing a beat, he said, "Look, it even cleans ties," and they chuckled a little. One of the administrators was a very dignified-looking gentleman with a goatee. He said to Billy, "How long have you been working with your father?" To which Billy replied, "All my life." They broke up in laughter, and the rest of the demonstration was cordial and very productive.

Dry Cleaners Were First

People in the dry cleaning business were the first to realize the advantages of our new system. Unlike many of the early inquirers, dry cleaners meant business when they called. Most of them were well established and either wrote a check for our equipment or financed it through their local bank.

In 1973, I was invited to speak at a meeting of the Indiana Dry Cleaners' Association at Indianapolis. The theme of the meeting was "DIVERSIFICATION." Dry cleaners were entering a period of extreme hardship and frustration, thanks to polyester leisure suits and hippies who didn't have their clothes cleaned. It was easy to see a major down turn coming, and the dry cleaning industry was looking for profitable ways to diversify. Everything from formal wear rental to necktie sales was being considered.

Carpet, upholstery and drapery cleaning were naturals for diversification since the dry cleaner was already considered a professional cleaner by consumers. Having a base of opera-

Bernie and Sonny Kress were among the early dry cleaners to go into the carpet cleaning business in 1972.

tion, an established clientele and office overhead already paid made this venture extremely attractive and unusually profitable. When the size of the investment is considered, entering the carpet cleaning business costs only a fraction of the amount it takes to open a dry cleaning plant. Several of the people at that meeting went into the business within the next few months.

Indiana dry cleaners who joined us in the early '70s were the Leonard family from Bloomington; Hunk Yarger, Marion; Bernie Kress, Jasper; Bud Surverkrup, Columbus; Dave Worl, Cambridge City; Jim Hutts, Clinton; Terry Moreland, Ft. Wayne; Paul Brill, Terre Haute; and Archie Hastings, Michigan City.

The Claypool family of Illinois and Don and Ruby Mitchell of Iowa were among the first out-of-state dry cleaners to realize the advantage of this added service to their business. We still see Scott Claypool and Don and Ruby Mitchell at our annual conventions.

Don Mitchell is quite a salesman and never misses an opportunity. While he was in my office, he noted that the drapes on my windows were less-than-aesthetically pleasing. He sold me new drapes, which he delivered all the way from Iowa. After the installation, he told me the drapes were made right down the street from us at the Aero Drapery plant in Indianapolis. But, I've never regretted the transaction. Don did a beautiful job and the drapes are still at my windows and look good.

Looking back on those early years, dry cleaners were attracted to our new system more than people already in the carpet cleaning business. During the next few years, hundreds of dry cleaners would make the move into carpet, upholstery and drapery cleaning. They are still among our best prospects and customers. They're a tough, resilient breed. Polyester leisure suits and hippies are gone, but now they have the EPA on their backs. Carpet cleaning must look better than ever to them now.

Truck-Mounts Begin to Sell

It was 1974 before I saw a competitive ad featuring truck-mounted equipment. Then these ads began to appear regularly in trade publications. Manufacturers in Oregon, California, and Arizona came out with their own versions of this new concept we had originated. The truck-mounted idea was finally catching on. As more people began to talk about truck-mounts, our sales increased.

People in the carpet cleaning business were finally listening to what we had to say, proving that the old adage was true: competition makes business. Sales increased steadily during the next few years. Today, the benefits, efficiency and economy of truck-mounted operation are taken for granted, and it is accepted as the ultimate method for carpet maintenance.

That was not the case in the early '70s.

The Numbers Game

Advertising in the cleaning industry, both the supply and the service side, is like feeding sharks. Competitors read ads and react as though they are having a feeding frenzy. Most will go one-up on anything a competitor says. A good example of this is the ad we ran in 1974 in a trade publication. It said that we used twice the pressure of the nearest competitor. We even put the pressure, 100 PSI (pounds per square inch), in the ad. We believed that was a strong selling point for our equipment since everyone else in the business at that time ran 35 to 45 PSI.

An early 1975 ad by a competitor read, "We use 200 PSI." Soon after that, someone else was touting 400 PSI, then 800 and 1,600. Recently I saw a brochure which claimed the capability of 2,650 PSI. This advertiser obviously had lost sight of our objective, which is to clean delicate carpet fibers, not remove gum from parking lots.

In recent years, there have been three manufacturers who claim to be Number One in the supply business. On the service side of the industry, the numbers game has always been a laughable issue. In Cleveland, Ohio, in the mid '70s, three carpet cleaning firms ran ads, each claiming to be Number One in that area.

These kinds of people must come in three's.

Horsepower and Hot Water

The same numbers game has developed concerning the temperature of the cleaning solution used in the industry. Temperature is advertised in the range of live steam. With some brands, the horsepower of the unit has been subjected to this "more is better" mentality. There even is diesel-powered cleaning equipment. Talk about using a shotgun to kill a mouse!

In the early '80s we began to advertise that we recovered more than 95 percent of the moisture we used in the cleaning process. Sure enough, a competitor beat us. I saw an ad in Minneapolis that claimed 110 percent recovery.

The following is a profound statement: "Publish a number and you will regret it." Someone will always beat you. If the price of a service is advertised, the numbers will go down. In equipment capability advertising, the numbers will go up.

We have never advertised a price for cleaning carpets, upholstery or draperies, even though that is a popular means of advertising in the cleaning business.

Disappointing Industry Meetings

With no distributors or dealers, it seemed like an impossible task to market our new truck-mounted concept to the rest of the industry. In the early '70s, our ads in trade publications brought responses that were not very productive.

In 1973, we decided to exhibit at two trade shows, thinking that this would be the way to reach the professional cleaner. The first show was in Columbus, Ohio, and was very disappointing. We took along fifty drums of our new powdered cleaning agent, thinking that we could sell it at the meeting. It seemed like everyone at that meeting was selling something and no one was buying anything. We had to haul all fifty drums back home again.

The other trade show we attended that year was in Cleveland, Ohio. There must have been about a hundred people at the hotel for the three-day convention. I thought this was a nice crowd and remember being right across the aisle from the Steamway exhibit and enjoying the friendly chides of Ralph Bloss. In those days Steamway made only portable equipment. I believe Ralph listened to our sales talk during the show because, not long afterwards, Steamway came out with a truck-mounted model.

Neither of us did well at that show, and on the last day Ralph said, "I'll tell you what, Bill. If you buy one of mine, I'll buy one of yours, and that way we can go home and say we didn't get skunked."

We didn't know it at the time, but one of the people who stopped by our booth would become a customer and long-term friend. Ken Hilbert was interested in starting a business when he visited our booth in Cleveland. He made the move in 1976, and today he and his family operate an extremely successful carpet, upholstery and drapery cleaning firm in Akron, Ohio. He was the only bright spot in that otherwise dull visit to Cleveland, Ohio.

My two sons were with me at that convention so I had time to survey the exhibitors and the audience. I counted sixty-seven salespeople. That left about thirty prospects, or more than two salesmen for every potential buyer. Some of the prospects were acting as shills for exhibitors, so this brought the potential even further down.

We went home very discouraged.

"Return to Sender"

That curt statement was more than a title to an Elvis Presley hit song. It became a common notation on brochures that we sent to people in the carpet cleaning business. We bought mailing lists of cleaning contractors and mailed literature on a regular schedule. The return mail was terrible. "Moved—Left No Forwarding Address," or, "Out of Business" were the cold, impersonal comments of the postal service. Stamped in a reddish maroon ink, it almost reminded one of dried blood. Somehow, the color seemed appropriate.

On two occasions in the early '70s, we bought marketing reports which showed a terrible attrition rate in the industry. Every mailing that we did substantiated those reports. This industry was losing nearly a third of its operators every year and yet was growing at a steady pace. The resulting turnover was tremendous. I just couldn't understand it since our own little service company was doing so well, and we had done it with very little promotion.

Ah, Ha!

Have you ever had one of those "Ah, ha!" experiences . . . as though someone has just turned on a light bulb in your head? "Ah, ha! Now I understand!" I had one of those in February of 1978. I attended an AIDS convention in Phoenix, Arizona. Now, before you get the wrong idea, this was AIDS, the association, not AIDS, the disease. The Association of Interior Decor Specialists (they have since changed their name) had a trade show at the Del Webb Hotel. As a member of AIDS, our service company received an invitation so I went as a cleaning contractor, not as an exhibitor. We had given up on exhibiting at trade shows after the one in Cleveland.

The Little Jewel

Strolling the aisles of the show in Phoenix one evening, I was doing what so many do. I was trying to avoid eye contact with the salesmen who were poised at the side of their booths. Passing one booth in particular was a challenge. The salesman was lying in wait and I could see that he was "locked in" on me. The booth right across the aisle from his was not attended so I focused on it as I tried to slip by. He came out into the aisle and got me.

Taking me by the arm, he said, "Hi, pal. Where're you from?" When I replied, "Indiana," you could almost hear him thinking out loud, "Watch me sell this hayshaker something." He was almost salivating as he led me into his booth. We walked over to a little plastic carpet cleaning machine, and he patted it lovingly as he began to talk about it.

I don't remember the brand name of the equipment, because never once during his presentation did he ever call it by brand name. He referred to it as "this little jewel," "that little jewel," or "my little jewel." The loving pats continued all through his sales presentation.

At one point, he said, "Pal, you take this little jewel back home with you to Indiana, plug ten bucks a room in the newspaper and you will blow your competition away." "Ten dollars?" I asked. "You mean I should clean carpets for ten dollars a room?" He fixed his steely eyes on me and said, "Yeah, pal! And you can do it, too. This little jewel will clean 5,000 square feet an hour."

Don't ever think for one moment that a liar has to wink, blink or do something to give away the fact that he has just told a whopper. This man was a professional. As I left his booth that evening, I had mixed emotions. I certainly had been entertained.

But then the reality of what I had heard began to descend upon me . . . 5,000 square feet an hour . . . I don't even walk that fast.

Then came the "Ah, ha!" experience. It hit me like a revelation. I wondered how many new people in the business, who didn't have the experience I did, had taken this man's suggestion and been infected with his advice about how to price their work. I began to understand our industry's terrible failure rate. Probably the greatest disservice a sales representative can render a prospect is to overstate the capabilities of a product.

Most failing or bait-and-switch businesses in the industry price by the room. And many of them advertise prices well below ten dollars. No one, especially a salesman, should tell anyone how to price a service. A price must be based on four factors: labor, material, overhead, and profit. These factors will determine the level of quality of the service.

Remember what I said about publishing a number?

How low can you go? Brett Bane helps Pawpaw show
some of the outlandish ads in the carpet cleaning business.

RUN 'N GUN
We Pay You $25
To Let Us Clean Your Carpet
You like qua...
so do we!
Call Ken
Offer expires June 1
Ken : 088-0987
BLOW 'N GO
TURKEY
TIME
SPECIAL
UNBELIEVABLE!
Free Carpet Cleaning
SCRUBBY DUB DUB
CARPET CLEANERS
Free
Scotchguarding
This is something
gobble about
LET US
JET 'N WET
SUDS AND SOAK
YOU
Name the Price
$
YOUR HOME
IS
YOUR OASIS
LET US
SETTLE YOUR
DUST
BIG!
BIG!!!!
SAVE 90% CALL JOE
AT
POWDER 'N PUFF
FOAM 'N FLUSH
Carpet Cleaning
$4.95
per room   3 rm. min.
FREE
TEFLON
We'll
Soak 'N Suck

V

Our Own Convention

Stop Moaning!

When the boys and I returned to Indianapolis in November from the 1973 Carpet Cleaners' Convention in Cleveland, we continued to moan about the show and how terrible we thought it was. After listening to us for awhile, Elizabeth finally suggested, "Why don't we have our own convention?"

We sent out invitations to our meager mailing list of equipment prospects and customers and on February 22 and 23, 1974, we had our very first convention. Fifty-six people attended, and we've had conventions, conferences and workshops ever since. In future years, the audience would be mostly Bane-Clene equipment and chemical customers.

Morris Cook of North Manchester, Indiana, was at that first convention. He owned a Von Schrader machine and bought one of ours later that year. Morris has retired, but his son Stuart has taken over the business. Ralph and Cindy Norris from Mount Summit, Indiana, were at that first meeting and became Bane-Clene system owners and good friends.

Ayres, Lazarus and Shillitos represented the department store industry at that first convention. We were really excited that such prominent people would take the time to come to hear what we had to say.

The Agenda

Most conventions in the industry have sessions on how to clean carpets. There are sophomoric contests on spotting.

*Bill Bane, Jr., setting up chairs
for the 1986 convention*

Others have races to see how quickly the contestants can set up for a job. Most trade shows take on a carnival atmosphere, complete with barkers.

Our feeling has always been that anyone can clean a carpet. Since we have a good training program, we decided that the theme of our conventions should be motivational and geared to getting business. Advertising, sales promotion, motivation and goal-setting, along with business management, would be the focus of our meetings.

Earl Nightingale, Dr. Herb True, Dr. Ken McFarland, Dick Semaan, Dick Gardner, Don Hudson, Bill Gove, Bud Wilkinson, Carl Erskine, Jonathon Trivers and many other famous speakers have addressed our group. Representatives of the Better Business Bureau, accountants, IRS agents, U.S. Department of Labor representatives, and lawyers have spoken at our meetings. Many speakers from the carpet industry have addressed Bane-Clene conventions over the years.

Without a doubt, the greatest man ever to speak to our group was Norman Vincent Peale. Dr. Peale was with us in 1980, 1983 and 1986. The audiences were the largest ever gathered at a convention in our industry. The excitement could be felt hours before his appearance.

Dr. Peale's speech in 1980 was so motivational that nearly every one of the firms represented that day grew and prospered during the next few years. Our own company made significant gains in the '80s as a result of some of his ideas. The power of positive thinking really works!

Annual meetings have become a focal point of friendship for people from around the world. Much of the motivation and inspiration comes from those who attend as they energize each other and share experiences.

Dr. Norman Vincent Peale spoke at three Bane-Clene conventions. He came to Indianapolis by himself in 1980. Mrs. Peale accompanied him to the conventions in 1983 and 1986.

Dr. Peale speaking at 1983 convention.

Dr. Herb True drove home a serious point in a humorous way at the 1976 convention.

Bob Schubert, replete in his Paul Revere costume, rode his horse up the center aisle at the 1976 convention.

*Earl Nightingale spoke at the
1977 convention.*

*Whatever I was saying, you can tell by Elizabeth's expression
that she isn't buying it!*

The 1979 convention featured these widely known speakers:

Dr. Kenneth McFarland

Nationally acknowledged as the most eloquent and effective exponent of what is commonaly referred to as the "American System" of our times.

Janet L. Atkinson

Ms. Atkinson was the first woman president of the Better Business Bureau of Central Indiana. Ms. Atkinson supported Bane-Clene in the "steam" controversy with the Council of BBB's.

Bill Gove

One of America's foremost platform personalities, Bill Gove has spent over thirty years addressing and thrilling American audiences. It is estimated he has fulfilled over 4,000 speaking engagements, including over 1,900 sales meetings and seminars.

Ned Hopper of the CRI spoke at three Bane-Clene conventions over the years.

*Bill Gove fires up the audience at the 1979 convention
on selling their services.*

*Jimmie, our resident leprechaun, shows fourth-
generation Matthew Bane how to clean carpet
at the 1979 convention.*

Dick Semaan gave one of the best presentations at the 1984 Bane-Clene convention about goal setting.

Famous football coach Bud Wilkinson spoke at the 1981 Bane-Clene convention.

Jimmie holds court at 1983 Bane-Clene convention.
Elizabeth's father became the national company mascot in 1975.
He passed away in 1986.

The famous "Gordon Pipers" of Indy "500" parade fame open the ceremonies for the 1983 Bane-Clene convention.

*L to R, Mrs. Peale, Dr. Peale, Elizabeth, Bill, Lois
and Brett at the Radisson Hotel, 1986 convention.*

*The "Murat Shrine Chanters" sang a patriotic
medley to open the 1986 convention.*

A new Chevy van, complete with a Mini-Mount system, was the door prize at the 1986 convention.

Ron Romine, Cincinnati, Ohio, reacts as his number is drawn to win the door prize at the 1986 convention.

Kay and Larry Domont of Bourbonnais, Illinois,
won truck and equipment in 1983.

Connie Bodine of Crawfordsville, Indiana,
won truck and equipment in 1984.

*Bane-Clene staff at the '86 convention in Indianapolis.
The door prize is in the background.*

*The banquet manager instructs the staff that served dinner for
Bane-Clene's guests at the 1991 convention. The Radisson Plaza
in Indianapolis has hosted several Bane-Clene meetings.*

Twenty-Five Years in Business

In 1986 we began a year-long celebration of our twenty-fifth year in business. We had a special coin struck of 99.9 percent pure silver by the Liberty Mint in Provo, Utah, and presented one to each company attending the convention. Dr. Peale was our keynote speaker; the door prize was a service vehicle complete with a truck-mounted cleaning unit worth more than $22,000.

The theme of the convention was "Sharing and Working Together." The fundamental practices that had made our company so successful were used as a format for the meeting. Many of the speakers were owners of Bane-Clene equipment.

Many of the speakers were owners of Bane-Clene equipment. They came to share their experiences with their peers in keeping with the theme of the meeting.

The ceremonies were opened by the Murat Shrine Chanters, who sang the national anthems of the United States and the United Kingdom. A medley of George M. Cohan tunes provided a rousing patriotic finale.

The significance of the celebration was emphasized by Dr. Peale, who reminded the audience that most businesses do not last long. In fact, the average life of a business in the United States is eight years, so we survived well beyond the norm.

A picnic under a huge tent, banquet, giant door prize, great speakers and lots of camaraderie were the order of business. And, without a doubt, one of the largest events ever staged in the cleaning industry was a parade during the 1986 meeting.

In an article in *The Cleaning Digest* (our company publication), I had asked everyone who lived close to Indianapolis to drive a service truck to the meeting at the Radisson Plaza Hotel. I thought it would be impressive to see thirty or forty carpet cleaning service trucks outside the hotel. Did I ever underestimate that turnout!

On Labor Day morning, we lined up to parade from the Radisson Plaza Hotel to our plant on Keystone Avenue. There were nearly two hundred trucks stretching for three miles on Keystone Avenue. Sheriff's cars and a motorcycle team from the Sheriff's Department escorted our convoy. Lt. Wilbert Tyler, who was in charge of security at our meeting, called for reinforcements when he saw the number of vehicles. The parade lasted for more than an hour.

1986 Parade

Lee Holst,
Master of Ceremonies
at 1986 convention

The Second Ride of Paul Revere

George Spurgeon, Bane-Clene's distributor in the United Kingdom, is a man who is seldom at a loss for words. But he was totally dumbfounded after he was introduced to speak at our convention in 1986. John Davis, an old friend who was dressed in a Paul Revere costume, came bursting into the rear of the convention hall. He was carrying a musket and ran down the aisle on one side of the room, across in front of the audience and

Paul Revere

The British

out the rear door on the other side.

He yelled at the top of his voice, "The British are coming, the British are coming, the British are coming!" George was flabbergasted and speechless for a full minute.

The Key to the City of Indianapolis

The Thirtieth Anniversary Convention had a dual purpose. In addition to celebrating thirty years in business, we dedicated a new building addition to our property. We had begun by purchasing a building at the corner of 40th Street and

Keystone Avenue and now owned the entire city block. Over a ten-year period, we had purchased all twelve properties down to 39th Street.

Mayor Stephen Goldsmith officiated at the ribbon-cutting ceremonies and presented the family with a beautiful gold key to the City of Indianapolis. We were overwhelmed by the number of people who made the trip to be with us on this very special occasion. More than 700 people came to our plant that day.

Monsignor Richard Kavanagh gave a beautiful invocation. Father Kavanagh was one of my teachers in high school and we play an occasional round of golf together. He is a terrific person and a great inspiration. Becky Barton sang our National Anthem and that of the United Kingdom.

None of us will ever forget that day.

Mayor Goldsmith cuts the ribbon to the new building addition at the 1992 convention.

More than 700 guests came in 1992 for the ribbon-cutting ceremony by the Mayor of Indianapolis. People came from all fifty states, the United Kingdom, the Virgin Islands, and Canada. Shaw Industries' display can be seen at right rear. Every major carpet and fiber producer was represented.

We Celebrate Quietly Every Year

The family celebrates every February 4th as our Founders' Day. A luncheon is usually the setting. Once in awhile, we go out for a more formal dinner. As I write this, we are planning our Thirty-Fifth Anniversary Celebration. I look forward to these events as a child looks forward to Christmas.

Elizabeth and I have always been sentimental about anniversary dates. When we were first married, we celebrated our one-month anniversary and it seemed as if the first year would never come to pass. On January 22, 1996, we celebrated the fiftieth anniversary of the evening we were introduced in Philadelphia.

The Good Lord willing, we will celebrate the fiftieth anniversary of our marriage on April 26, 1997.

L to R, Elizabeth, Monsignor Richard Kavanagh, Bill Bane

Bill, Jr., presented a plaque to Dr. Leeds at the 1992 convention. Dr. Leeds was our first customer and remained a good customer until his death in 1995.

VI

Mini-Clinics

Border-to-Border and Coast-to-Coast

In 1974, after the success of our first convention, we began conducting one-day seminars, called Mini-Clinics. For the next fifteen years, these were held in hotels from border-to-border and coast-to-coast. The meetings were about our service company and proved to be extremely popular with audiences everywhere. They all liked to hear about our business experiences, and it gave us the opportunity, in the process, to show our equipment and chemical line. This approach was very well received in a cleaning community that was hardened by high-pressure salespeople.

Bill Bane speaking at a Mini-Clinic in 1978.

One of the main points I would drive home during a Mini-Clinic was that anyone who was **sold** something was less likely to succeed than the person who **bought** a product. While these may sound similar, there is a huge difference. Someone who buys a product because he is convinced it is the best, and that he will be the best because of it, is far ahead of the person who is sold something by a slick salesperson. After a period of buyer's remorse, there is always a doubt in the back of the customer's mind that the decision was wrong. Even a small doubt can become a big handicap in business.

During the fifteen years I held Mini-Clinics, I spoke to thousands of cleaners in hundreds of locations. On a West Coast swing we would have as many as ten meetings in twenty days and travel more than 6,000 miles. Short runs in the Midwest would see us do nine meetings in ten days. Sometimes we would make a loop of three meetings and cover about 700 miles.

I preferred a motor home for travel since most of our meeting sites were in remote areas and small towns off the beaten path. The exceptions, of course, were meetings in Alaska, Hawaii, and the United Kingdom.

We began with a small mini-motor home, graduated to

GMC Motor Coach

Diesel Motor Coach

Len Lepak operated the furniture cleaning plant at Ayres' warehouse and doubled as a bus driver on the Mini-Clinic circuit.

a GMC coach and eventually bought a large diesel motor coach. Many times we rolled all night between meetings.

Len Lepak, who ran our furniture cleaning plant, went with me to many of the meetings. He was a good driver and a big help in setting up meeting rooms. Len retired in 1979, but still went on the road with me for the next few years. Elizabeth, Oka, Len and I would stay for hours after a Mini-Clinic to talk with people who had come to ask questions about our service business.

Cross Section of the Industry

At every meeting we met new prospects for our equipment and chemicals. Many of them became customers and friends. There was only one meeting that I considered a complete failure. At a Holiday Inn in Columbia, South Carolina, our entire audience consisted of two people. One was a HydraMaster salesman and the other was a Duraclean franchise representative. That was the longest meeting we ever had. At least it seemed that way.

The next smallest audience we ever had consisted of three people representing two companies. It was at the Holiday Inn in Hays, Kansas, in 1978. We did a lot better there. Both companies purchased a system, which made it our best meeting, percentagewise. One man has since passed away, but Clyde Puckett, who attended the meeting with another member of his company, is still very much an associate. We have the opportunity to see him and his wife Brenda occasionally.

Most meetings drew between thirty and fifty people. Our largest Mini-Clinic audience was in Philadelphia in 1981. That meeting was attended by 126 people. There was a good cross section of our prospective market at that meeting. Carpet cleaners, janitorial firms, dry cleaners, carpet retailers and department store representatives made up the audience.

Inferiority Complex

It was difficult for me to speak to an audience when I first began the Mini-Clinics. I had a deep-seated fear that I would look amateurish. After all, I was exposed to veterans of the cleaning business, and I hadn't been in it very long.

My fears were quickly put to rest. I found genuinely interested people, confused by the myriad of sales claims and truly anguished by the quality of the equipment, chemicals and training available to them. For the most part, they were very kind, and I got to meet the rank and file of the industry on their own turf.

Mini-Clinics gave us the opportunity to present an honest program outlining not only the positive side of the business, but also dealing heavily with the negative side. Professional sales people are trained to accentuate the positive and eliminate the negative. I have always felt that being honest and pointing out the pitfalls in the business is very important in achieving success.

People seemed to appreciate my talking openly about the many problems which face a service operator. And I knew these problems very well.

Respectful Audience?

Audiences were, for the most part, very respectful. Only on one occasion was I just a little fearful. In Franklin, Tennessee, a big man in dirty coveralls came to our meeting. He sat ominously in the front row. Rude and extremely hostile, he became incensed when I began to talk about our method in comparison to the rotary shampoo system, which he obviously favored.

He had been in the lounge of the Holiday Inn before the meeting and apparently had too much to drink. He took over the meeting for a few minutes and became very threatening. My son, Donnie, removed him from the audience, and the rest of the group seemed apologetic for his behavior.

One time in Chicago I was talking about the advantages of direct mail advertising. A man in the audience stood up and said, "I don't know how you can say good things about junk mail. It's the most expensive form of advertising there is."

I agreed that all advertising is expensive, hoping that he would cease. But, he kept the floor.

"A lot of mailmen throw junk mail down the nearest sewer," he went on. I agreed with him again and acknowledged that this had indeed happened. I was sure that agreeing with him on this issue would shut him up. But, he stayed on his feet and continued, "The very worst thing about junk mail is that when people get it in their mailboxes, what do they do with it? They take one look at it and throw it away."

I agreed with him again. But, this time I asked him a question: "How did you happen to hear about this meeting?" He took a brochure from his coat pocket and said. "I got this brochure from you in the mail." The audience laughed and he sheepishly slid down into his seat, not to be heard from again.

Direct mail does work.

Fake Water?

We had just finished doing a demonstration at a Mini-Clinic in Cleveland, Ohio, back in 1979. Donnie had made forty passes over the same spot on the carpet with the solution valve depressed to show that it was nearly impossible to over wet carpet with our system.

When we finished the demonstration, I ceremoniously turned the carpet sample over to show that the back was dry and then passed it around so the audience could see that the face fibers were wet. A woman in the audience watched with great interest and then uttered, "I'll bet you used fake water."

Barracuda

Our 1975 convention was at the Atkinson Hotel in downtown Indianapolis. I looked out my hotel room window on the second morning and saw five truck-mounted units on the parking lot. I hasten to add that these were not Bane-Clene units. Salesmen had set up shop and were demonstrating to the people who had come to our convention. I must admit I was pretty upset.

Later in the day one of our speakers, Benjamin M. Burr of Hercules Fibers, mentioned the parking lot salesmen at the beginning of his speech. He said, "Bill, I know that you, and many of the people here at the convention, are upset about those parking lot salesmen who were out there this morning. Don't be! Those barracuda are a sure sign of success. They only follow successful people because they can't rip off a failure."

That was the beginning of my education in understanding and appreciating competition.

Iowa City, Iowa

In June of 1979 we were at a Mini-Clinic in a Holiday Inn in Iowa City. It was hot that Saturday afternoon. The hotel had rented our meeting room to someone else, and we had to put

A typical Mini-Clinic crowd.

about forty people in a room that would comfortably hold twenty. To add insult to injury, the air conditioner failed during the meeting.

I was telling the group about Ben Burr and his comments about the barracuda when a man in the rear of the room jumped up and ran outside. His face was beet-red. I thought he was having a heat stroke since the room was so hot. At the intermission, there he was on the parking lot, demonstrating a truck-mounted machine to some of the people who were at our meeting. In letters a foot high on the side of his truck was the word "BARRACUDA."

The Butler folks did the same thing at Holyoke, Massachusetts. They had two of their direct-drive units on the parking lot of the Holiday Inn the last time I was there. Numerous others have taken advantage of our ability to draw an audience.

We appreciate them all.

Market Research?

After each meeting I had the opportunity to meet people one-on-one and discuss their individual situations. Often these informal sessions would last for hours. In Denver, Colorado, I talked with one man for seven hours, finally leaving him after midnight.

People would openly discuss their problems, hopes and desires. They seemed genuinely pleased that someone would listen to them. I learned more about our industry at these informal meetings than a research institute could have learned with a $5 million government grant.

Bane-Clene Mini-Clinics were held in various hotels around the country. The beautiful Red Lion Inn in San Jose, California, and the brand new Crowne Plaza in the suburbs of Washington, D.C., were probably the nicest as far as accommodations were concerned. But the winner for good service was the old Holiday Inn in Davenport, Iowa. Even though the facilities were obviously old, they were clean and well maintained, and the people who worked there were the best trained and the most courteous hotel employees we saw.

VII

Speech Making

Invited Speaker

On several occasions I have accepted invitations to speak at industry functions. In 1978, I delivered the keynote address for a meeting of the California Cleaners' Institute in San Diego. It was a large meeting, and I felt extremely honored that I was invited to be the keynote speaker.

I was nervous about speaking to this group since it was one of the premier associations in the industry and drew a large attendance. Dick Maplesden and his wife, Jackie, who were active members of CCI, took Elizabeth and me across the border into Mexico for dinner and an evening of Mexican entertainment. All of the officers and members of the association made us feel quite comfortable. Howard Olansky of *Installation and Cleaning Specialist* magazine and Bob Hughes, the President of Chemspec, took us to dinner on the evening after I spoke.

Ed York, who needs no introduction to anyone who has been in the business a few years, came up to me after my speech and said, "If someone could only speak like you and have my brains, they could get rich in this business." I think that was as near a compliment as one is likely to get from Mr. York. He and I have been at odds over some industry issues; however, I have always had a certain amount of respect for him as an innovator and organizer.

I think Ed must have felt the same way about me. At least he didn't get up and walk out on my speech as he did in the middle of Mike West's acceptance speech as new President of the CCI. Halfway through Mike's speech, Ed and his entourage left. They were all seated together in the center of the audience and caused quite a stir in getting to the aisle. Mike was obviously quite annoyed. He stopped and waited until they were gone.

The audience in San Diego was very courteous and generous with their applause, but my pleasure was dampened considerably when a lady came up to the lectern and put a note in front of me. It read, "Please cut it short; we're running late." I was just ready to give my punch line, which was a quote by Earl Nightingale. I got it backwards and had to correct myself.

Chicago

Howard Olansky asked me to speak in Chicago at the Merchandise Mart and take part in a panel discussion. It was in January of 1980 and the windy city was cold. The audience was small and just about as cold as the weather. Fritz Rench, the chairman of Host (Racine Industries, Inc.) was on the program with me. Considering the fact that our methods of cleaning are so different, it was a cordial meeting. Both of us conducted ourselves as gentlemen, and we took questions from the audience after our talks. Several steam cleaners in the audience were a little rough

Howard Olansky, editor and publisher of three major industry trade magazines.

on Fritz, but he handled their questions with a great deal of tact and defended his products very well.

Craig Jasper, a cleaner from the Chicago area who had been to our school in Indianapolis was at the meeting and came up to Elizabeth to show her a new chart he had made for figuring the square footage of a room. He said that he had the help of a mathematician and an accountant in designing this new work aid. Elizabeth took one look at the chart and said, "Isn't that funny? They both made the same mistake I did when I made our chart!"

Imitation is the sincerest form of flattery, so we took the purloining of our chart as a compliment.

On Top of the Mountain

One of the nicest experiences I've ever had in public speaking was in Pennsylvania. I accepted an invitation to give the keynote address for the Tri State Carpet Cleaners' Association. The meeting was at Seven Springs Resort in the mountains of Western Pennsylvania.

Walt (Ozzie) Werner, the president of the group, met me at the Pittsburgh airport and took me to his home, where I met his family. He gave me a tour of his cleaning plant and really made me feel welcome. We drove up to the mountains later that day, and I was treated to a dinner hosted by officers of the association. Al South of DuPont and Walt Lipscomb of Allied Fibers accompanied me to their hospitality suites and introduced me to many of the members of the association.

I remember sitting on the little balcony of my suite and watching skiers come down the slopes. It was a delightful spot, and the audience the next day gave me a standing ovation when

I finished my speech. Outside of Bane-Clene conventions, this was the warmest, most receptive audience I've ever had.

Toledo, Ohio

In 1993, my old friend Herb Harpham asked me to give the keynote speech for the United Carpet Cleaners' Institute at their convention in Toledo, Ohio. I've known and respected Herb since we met in the late '60s. He is Vice-President of Sales for Certified Chemicals.

Herb and his lovely wife, Jan, took Elizabeth and me to dinner the night before I spoke. He told a great story about one of the suppliers who was exhibiting at the trade show. Herb was in charge of the program. Ralph Bloss stormed up to him and said, "Who in the hell invited Bane to speak at this meeting?" Herb had to admit that it was he who was the culprit. Later, however, Ralph condescended to shake hands with me.

Kathy Zimmermann, the president of the association, was a charming hostess and took Elizabeth and me to each booth to meet the exhibitors. The audience was very gracious and courteous during my speech.

Between a President and an Astronaut

In 1977 Bill Dorrell, my erstwhile Yellow Pages representative, asked me to come to a luncheon for Yellow Pages salespeople. He said, "If you don't mind, maybe you could say a few words about Yellow Pages." That sounded innocuous enough.

It was on the day after our annual convention, and I really hadn't had time to think about it. On top of that, I didn't feel well that day, and I told Elizabeth that I didn't think I would go. She said, "Now, you promised Bill that you would do it, so please go."

The luncheon was at the Elks' Club, and when I arrived, I had difficulty finding a parking space. On entering, I was handed an engraved program, and there I was listed as a formal speaker right before the president of Indiana Bell Telephone Company and after Gene Cernan, the famous astronaut. The place was packed, and I have never quite forgiven Dorrell for not warning me about the celebrities and large attendance at the meeting.

At the first intermission, I begged a 3" x 5" card at the registration desk, went to the rest room and jotted down a few thoughts about my experiences with Yellow Pages. I can't remember what I said, but the audience was very kind with their applause, and afterward even Bill Dorrell said it was a good speech.

Bane-Clene Conventions

I gave my first speech at our 1974 convention and have addressed each convention since that time. My son Donnie, who is the treasurer of our company, says that a keynote speaker should not know the meaning of the words fear, intimidation or honorarium, especially honorarium.

Donnie likes for me to deliver the keynote address because, unlike professional speakers, I work free.

One of our panels.

Convention crowd.

VIII

The Great Steam Controversy

Kill the New Method

Business did not come easy for steam cleaners in the early '70s. Dry foam, shampoo and powder manufacturers, along with some prominent franchise operators, did their best to assassinate this new phenomenon called "steam cleaning."

A petition was circulated by competitors in the State of Wisconsin, which resulted in the banning of the word "steam" in Yellow Pages advertising in that state. It is noteworthy to mention that both Host (Racine Industries, Inc.) and Von Schrader Manufacturing Company are located in that state.

Duraclean and ServiceMaster franchises ran negative ads in all parts of the country. They coined such phrases as "no steaming," "no boiling," "no shrinking." Consumer groups were bombarded with requests to stop this misrepresentation of calling our process "steam."

Negative petitions about steam cleaning were circulated among Von Schrader Associates throughout the nation. After a year of this barrage, the Council of Better Business Bureaus in Washington, D.C., issued an edict proclaiming that the use of the word "steam" was indeed misrepresentation. Some local bureaus issued negative statements about steam cleaning.

Things looked pretty bleak as 1973 drew to a close.

The Steam Carpet Cleaners' Association (SCCA)

In early 1974, I organized the Steam Carpet Cleaners' Association, whose main purpose was to fight the injustices being directed toward our method of cleaning. One of our staunch supporters was Janet Atkinson, President of the Central Indiana Better Business Bureau.

Another supporter was Sol Petruzzi of L. S. Ayres and Company, who used his influence to bring Max Gruetzner of DuPont into the matter. Max encouraged me to form an association and was active in the group.

During the next three years the membership of SCCA grew to 1,003, and we spearheaded the offensive against the Council of Better Business Bureaus, the Federal Trade Commission and all of the opposition who were constantly agitating the situation.

Until that time, the SCCA was the only organization in the history of the carpet cleaning industry to bring more than 1,000 individual firms together for any purpose. This was an accomplishment all in itself.

The St. Louie Blues

The Better Business Bureau in St. Louis, Missouri, joined with KMOX-TV in a campaign against advertising by steam cleaners. I was invited to attend a meeting at the offices of the Better Business Bureau in St. Louis in 1975.

When I arrived, it looked more like an inquisition than a meeting. Julius Hunter from KMOX-TV was there, replete with lights and camera. There were at least ten people around the massive table in the board room. It was a frightening experience and I thank God for giving me the strength and courage to stay.

After Mr. Hunter prefaced the meeting with a few comments, I was asked to give the position of the SCCA. I began by thanking all of those present for allowing us the opportunity and then I looked at the president of the bureau and said, "As I came in, I noticed all of those file cabinets in the other room. I know they must be filled with complaints about steam cleaners from consumers in St. Louis. I won't ask you to bring all of them in, but would you let me examine just one consumer-originated complaint so I can comment more intelligently about it?"

There was dead silence in the room. The only noise was the humming of the TV camera. Just one consumer complaint is all I asked for. They didn't have one. I then pointed out that the entire situation had been instigated by complaints from dry foam cleaners and a local franchise.

That evening, Julius Hunter called off the campaign during his television news show and, indeed, treated us in a very complimentary manner. This same strategy worked later that year in Louisville, Kentucky, with the Better Business Bureau in that city. Competitors were doing all of the complaining, not consumers.

Contrary to common belief, steam carpet cleaning was not new and had been around for one hundred years. At our 1976 convention, a bookmark was introduced which had been printed for Howard's Steam Carpet Cleaning of Indianapolis, which was founded in 1876. The bookmark had been found in an old dictionary, and a reproduction was made of it and distributed at the convention. (See following page)

In early 1977, Chuck Hudson, who operated a carpet cleaning service in Maryland and was a member of SCCA, went with me to call on Kenneth Orr. Mr. Orr was an attorney with the Council of Better Business Bureaus in Washington, D.C.

A word to the Good Housewife.

Upon sanitary as well as economic principles, all carpets should be taken up and cleaned at least once a year. It should never be reckoned as an expense, for they will last twice as long if kept free from dirt and moth and there will be a great saving of doctor's bills. An eminent physician and health officer says that "few people realize that the defilement of the air they breathe, that causes numerous diseases, is due to neglected carpets. The patterns are bright and alluring and the textures soft and luxurious, concealing the minute disease-breeding dust which rises so readily."

RENOVATING.

We have a valuable process for scouring and renovating. If the carpets are soiled with soot, grease, or any kind of stain, this process removes them, and at the same time makes the colors fast and brings them out clear and bright without blending, leaving the carpet as sweet and clean as when new. It also acts as moth preventive.

The cleansing and renovation of carpets, etc., damaged by fire, smoke or water, a specialty. Inspection of this part of the work earnestly desired.

We reiterated the experiences I had in St. Louis and Louisville and presented evidence that all of the complaining about steam cleaning was being done by competitors.

Chuck Hudson

Mr. Orr listened intently, then sat back in his chair and said, "I'm really tired of hearing about all of this. I ought to dump the whole mess into the lap of the FTC [Federal Trade Commission]. If you people can't get your industry together, I think

Gury Poletajev, Technical Director at Burlington Industries, has spoken at three Bane-Clene conventions. He represented carpet manufacturers at the SCCA meeting in Philadelphia in 1977.

that's what I'll do." This threat prompted us to organize a meeting to address the problem and to build a consensus in the industry quickly.

Running Out Of Steam

In October of 1977, the Steam Carpet Cleaners' Association sponsored a conference in Philadelphia. Many prominent people in the cleaning industry attended, as well as government officials, BBB representatives and members of the carpet industry.

One of the principal benefactors was Irv Shaw, who was with the Jute Carpet Backing Council. Bob Coleman, who was at that time Executive Director of the Association of Interior Decor Specialists, participated. Gury Poletajev, the Director of Technical Services for Burlington Industries, spoke at the meeting. Howard Olansky of *Installation and Cleaning Specialist* magazine threw his weight behind the effort and was responsible for much of the publicity about the meeting.

At that meeting, I read a statement that Max Gruetzner had given us in 1974. It was a scientific definition for the word "steam." He said, "Steam is any discernible water vapor and may exist over an infinite range of pressures and temperatures." He used "cold steam vaporizers," which are used in hospitals,

*Maxwell K. Gruetzner, Chemical Engineer from DuPont,
spoke at five Bane-Clene conventions.*

as one of many examples of steam in other than boiling or super-heated form.

When his statement was read to the audience in Philadelphia, for all intents and purposes the issue was resolved. The Council of Better Business Bureaus rescinded its directive later that year.

During the two years following the meeting in Philadelphia, steam carpet cleaning operations mushroomed throughout the land. With this explosive growth came charlatans who took advantage of the popularity of steam cleaning with the consumer. Its reputation began to suffer and decline. The trend continues even to this day, as nearly every bait-and-switch advertiser touts steam cleaning.

IX

Endorsement by the Carpet Makers

The Beginning of Operation ABC

In my speech to the Bane-Clene convention in March of 1980, you could have heard a pin drop when I said we should all stop using the word "steam" in our advertising and use the term "The Bane-Clene Way" instead. Many people asked me why, after all those years of fighting for the use of the word "steam," I would recommend not using it. Had I lost my senses?

While it was true that not many people knew the name "Bane-Clene," at least they didn't know anything bad about Bane-Clene. That was not the case with steam. After the settlement of the dispute with the Council of Better Business Bureaus, a hoard of charlatans rushed into the business and the reputation of anyone who used "steam" in advertising material was in jeopardy.

That convention was the beginning of Operation ABC (Awareness of Bane-Clene). In June of that year, still fired up by Dr. Peale's great motivational speech, a group of sixty Bane-Clene equipment owners met in Indianapolis to organize a new association. They wanted to be an exclusive group which would be the epitome of ethics and represent the highest quality in workmanship.

In a strategy session, someone suggested that we embark on a national television advertising program. Since there were no funds available for consumer-oriented advertising, it was decided that we would seek the endorsement of carpet

110

manufacturers. This seemed like a logical place to start consumer education. We started writing to manufacturers, sending them our *Cleaning Digest* and making regular trips to carpet mills. This was a painfully slow process. It took nearly four years for the new program to have any positive results.

The First Cheer Leader

In August of 1983, Jim Keener of J&J Industries inquired about a brochure we had sent him. J&J is one of the most respected manufacturers of commercial carpeting. Donnie and I went to Dalton to do a demonstration for Jim and to sell him on the idea that he should recommend our small, but growing, network of people to his customers.

After the demonstration, Jim said, "Bill, I like the job Don did, but can you guarantee that I would get the same quality of work on the West Coast that I got here today?" I told him that I couldn't guarantee that, but I would guarantee that the people we recommended would be only those who used our equipment and chemicals. They also would have attended our school, be certified by Bane-Clene Institute and would have signed a pledge of integrity.

Jim Keener was asked to speak at our 1984 convention. During his speech, he gave us a public endorsement and introduced a new brochure that recommended "The Bane-Clene Way" and featured our toll-free telephone number. His company was the first of many to utilize this service. Needless to say, Jim got a standing ovation from the partisan audience. He has been an outspoken advocate of "The Bane-Clene Way" ever since.

In 1991, Shaw Endorsement, the largest manufacturer of carpets in the world, published carpet maintenance brochures

Bill Bane thanks Jim Keener of J&J Industries for being the first carpet maker to endorse the Bane-Clene system.

under the brand names of "Philadelphia," "Stratton," and "Shaw Commercial Carpets." In each brochure the Bane-Clene toll-free telephone number was listed for the consumer to locate the nearest authorized Bane-Clene operator. Shaw has listed our phone number in all subsequent maintenance brochures for their many brand names and also in their warranty literature.

Did We Make the Right Decision?

That ten-year period from 1980 to 1990 was probably the most excruciating era in the history of Bane-Clene. We took a chance and stopped advertising to the cleaning trade. Most of our advertising budget was devoted to carpet manufacturers and retailers. Ads asked them to call us for the phone number of their nearest authorized Bane-Clene representative.

There were many internal and external pressures to stop advertising to the carpet manufacturers and return to the trade magazines. Our own sales department lobbied for such a move. The trade press was adamant in trying to convince me I had made the biggest mistake of my life.

Some of our budget was spent in *Better Homes and Gardens*, a consumer magazine. We bought regional ads and did some selective mailing to specific target markets. There was no chance in that advertising for instant profit for our company. The strategy was to generate a strong referral program. Our individual operators would get stronger and expand their operations. We would profit by supplying them, as opposed to selling equipment to their competitors.

This was the trickle-down theory in its purest form . . . but, in reverse.

Pilgrimages to Dalton

Johnny Loggins of Dawsonville, Georgia, demonstrates for carpet mill representatives. Every major carpet mill was represented at this meeting in Dalton, Georgia.

Since the early eighties, we have held regular meetings in Dalton, Georgia. Some were sparsely attended. I remember one meeting where five of us from Bane-Clene put on a demonstration for Dave Schell, the one lone individual in the audience. That was embarrassing.

Most of our meetings in Dalton, however, consisted of large crowds. We were always cordially received by members of the carpet industry. They seemed to appreciate that someone was finally talking about maintaining the floor covering they made.

At one of our meetings, there must have been seventy or eighty representatives from the carpet industry in attendance. We were excited by the large audience. I stood in the front of the room giving the opening remarks, and then I asked that the audience watch a fifteen-minute video tape about our service company back in Indiana. No sooner had I made the announcement than a man left the meeting room with this statement ringing in everyone's ears, "I don't have time to waste watching TV."

It was a frightening moment, but I had the presence of mind to smile and explain that I thought the audience would be interested in how a legitimate service company works. I wanted to establish the fact that we were indeed in the business and not like so many other sales organizations that really didn't know what the service industry was all about.

Tom Durkan, Sr., who left in such a huff, was the president of a carpet mill, so we were very disappointed. But, a week later, Jackie Kinsey of Durkan called my office and said he wanted to use our service throughout the nation. Mr. Durkan is a busy man who drives right to the point and I have always found him to be very direct, sometimes to the point of creating

*Don Terry, company chemist, talks to audience
of carpet manufacturers.*

fear. His company is a good customer for hundreds of our operators who participate in Operation ABC.

Believe me, we really earned that one.

"Surfaces"

One of the largest events in the carpet industry is held in Las Vegas, Nevada, each year. The show is called "Surfaces" and is attended by thirty to forty thousand carpet retailers. There are nearly seven hundred exhibitors, and my company has been one of those since 1991.

Prior to "Surfaces," we exhibited at several Neocon events in Chicago as well as at the Atlanta Carpet Market for seven consecutive years. These exposures to the carpet retailer have proven to be extremely valuable.

We meet three types of carpet retailers at these shows: those who are interested in getting into the cleaning business; those who are interested in cleaning but do not want to be in the business; and those who are totally disinterested in the cleaning and maintenance of their products. Believe it or not, there are more of the last group. The disinterested retailer does not stop and talk with us, but the other two types do stop to listen to what we have to say.

Those who want to be in the business are given information about our system, training and advertising programs. The others who stop by are told about our "Network of Excellence," Operation ABC. They are given literature that describes how to contact the nearest certified Bane-Clene operator in the hope that an affiliation will be established. This is a true win/win situation.

ABC Pays Off

The referral idea has worked so well that today we have a computerized national program. Fifty-three carpet makers endorse, recommend or use "The Bane-Clene Way." Our toll-free number is distributed to hundreds of thousands of consumers in the maintenance brochures published by these forward-thinking manufacturers. The consumer has only to tell us his zip code, and he is quickly referred to the nearest member of Operation ABC, our "Network of Excellence."

Most executives in the carpet industry shy away from using the word "endorse." Many of their legal advisors fear an implied warranty when such a term is used. Some mills prefer to say they recommend our method. Others only grudgingly admit that they use our referral service. We really don't care what they call us or how they rationalize the fact that they use our service.

The important thing is that they "Call 'Us' on the Carpet."

Some of the major carpet manufacturers who endorse, recommend, or use
The Bane-Clene "Network of Excellence"

Barrett Carpet Mills, Inc.
Beaulieu of America, Inc.
Blue Ridge Carpet Mills
C & A (Collins & Aikman)
Cabin Crafts Carpets
Carriage Industries, Inc.
Columbus Mills, Inc.
Conquest Carpet Mills, Inc.
Coronet Carpets, Inc.
Cumberland Mills, Inc.
CV Carpets, Ltd.
D&W Carpet &
    Rug Co.,Inc.
Daltonian Carpet &
    Cushion, Inc.
Diamond Rug &
    Carpet Mills, Inc.
Dimension Carpet
Dorsett Carpet Mills, Inc.
Durkan Patterned
    Carpet, Inc.
E.T.C. Carpet Mills, Ltd.
Evans & Black Carpets
Galaxy Carpet Mills, Inc.
General Felt Industries,Inc.
Gradus Carpets, Ltd.
The Harbinger Co., Inc.
Hollytex Carpet Mills, Inc.
Horizon Industries, Inc.
Interloom International

J&J Industries, Inc.
J&L Carpets, Inc.
Lees Commercial Carpets
Lowe's Carpet Corporation
Mannington Carpets, Inc.
Masland Carpets, Inc.
Mohawk Industries, Inc.
Networx
Patcraft
Philadelphia Carpets
Prince Street
    Technologies, Ltd.
Richmond Carpet Mills, Inc.
Salem Carpets
Shaw Commercial Carpets
Shaw Industries, Inc.
ShawMark Carpets
Shaw Rugs
Specialty Carpets, Inc.
Sponge-Cushion, Inc.
Stratton
Summit Carpet
    Manufacturing Co., Ltd
Sunrise Carpet
    Industries, Inc.
Sutton Carpets
U.S. Axminster, Inc.
Whitecrest Carpet Mills
World Carpets, Inc.
WundaWeve Carpets, Inc.

X

The Chemical Business

The Sudsy, Soapy Mentality

There was no intention on our part to go into the chemical business. Early in our new carpet cleaning operation, however, it became painfully evident that the chemical industry was not responding to the needs of the new steam cleaning method. They were still locked into the "shampoo" era and sold cleaning agents that foamed even when gently agitated by the pressure of the water.

Carpets which had previously been shampooed or dry-foamed were a particular problem. When we wet them and agitated the pile with water pressure, we might easily have ended up standing in foam to our ankles.

To fully understand the soap residue problem, try emptying a liquid soap container . Thoroughly dry it, then put a little water in it and slightly agitate it. It will fill with suds. Empty those suds out, rinse and dry it, and do the same experiment again. There will be suds again, and in an empty container. Picture a carpet tuft that is saturated with soap and the problem becomes apparent.

The residue was nearly impossible to get out on the first try and wicking caused us great grief. Blue carpets might turn a shade of brown, and grey carpets sometimes took on a faint pink hue as the sudsy residue wicked up to the surface during the drying period. As the last drop of moisture evaporated into the air, a trace of any mineral or chemical that was in the water remained on the tip of the carpet fiber. We really needed help, and none of the chemical manufacturers listened to our pleas.

The trade associations knew nothing about the problems we were experiencing. In fact, the few associations at that time were controlled by established cleaning firms that operated cleaning plants and were totally opposed to on-location cleaning. The few that did clean on-location used rotary shampoo machines. Chemical manufacturers naturally catered to them since they represented the status quo in the cleaning industry.

So, we went into the chemical business.

Our Own Juice

Don Terry, who is now a vice-president with Bane-Clene, was hired as a consulting chemist in 1973. He developed original formulas that answered our needs concerning foaming, wicking, browning and short dwell time. Supplying our own service company and those who owned our equipment gave us the customer base we needed.

Over the years, Don has continued to upgrade and improve our chemical line. He guided us through the very difficult time when fifth-generation or stain resistant fibers, as they are known, were introduced to the carpet market.

Donald W. Terry, Sr., Vice-President and Bane-Clene's graduate chemist.

Stainmaster Carpets

In the fall of 1986, DuPont introduced Stainmaster fibers to the consumer. They crashed upon the scene with little Ricky throwing his plate of food onto the carpet in a series of television commercials. A magic sponge would appear, wave across the surface of the carpet and the food would disappear. It was a brilliant advertising campaign on which DuPont reportedly spent $50 million. A lethargic carpet industry was kicked into a higher gear as sales increased dramatically.

I wrote to the Public Relations Department of DuPont in the fall of 1986 and asked if there were any special cleaning instructions necessary for the new product. I never received an answer. In January of 1987, Elizabeth and I went to L. S. Ayres and bought the new Stainmaster product so we could experiment on it and find out for ourselves how it reacted to cleaning. We knew that with the amount of money DuPont was spending on advertising, sales would be substantial and we wanted to be ready to clean the fiber.

The Stevens product we purchased, containing the Stainmaster fiber, has acquitted itself extremely well. It was installed in our family room, which has an entrance off our garage. The traffic lane is right through the center of the room into our kitchen. The location does not lend itself to rearranging furniture to change the traffic pattern. The color is Camel Haze, a particularly light color, and was selected on purpose so it would show as much soil as possible.

The plush pile was selected even though it was a poor choice for this location. It has been abused by salad spills, pizza, dogs, cats, kids and lots of foot traffic. We have put every conceivable after-market treatment on it and it has been cleaned hundreds of times in the testing process. There is no noticeable change in the tip definition of the fibers or change in the color.

But, we didn't know any of that back in early 1987. Later that year, information began to make its way into the cleaning industry that the new miracle fiber did indeed need special attention. Maintenance, apparently, had not been considered by the marketing department at DuPont.

The Spot Where the Outhouse Once Stood

As the time neared to clean the new products, DuPont hurriedly appointed Stanley Steemer as their official warranty service representative. A roar arose from professional cleaners across the land that was heard back in Wilmington, Delaware. Editorials in trade publications blasted DuPont. One editor even went so far as to say, " DuPont has built their relationship with the cleaning industry on the spot where the outhouse once stood." Never in the history of the industry has such mass dissatisfaction been displayed.

I took a position, editorially, that this was still America and that DuPont had every right to deal with whomever they wished. This was not a popular position among my peers and brought considerable hate mail and a few blistering phone calls.

The Peace Maker

During the next two years, the reality of cleaning the product and making peace with the professional cleaning community would fall on the shoulders of William E. Doan, a DuPont executive. He spent all of his time traveling and speaking to carpet cleaners around the country. He was ably assisted by Cy Gantt, a gentleman of high quality and great public relations skill.

Cy invited Bane-Clene personnel to DuPont for tours of the fiber facility at Seaford, Delaware, and the telephone operation in Wilmington. Elizabeth and I were treated to a fabulous reception at the DuPont Country Club. I even got to play golf on the famous DuPont golf course with Caren McCabe, a DuPont executive. Elizabeth had been in Caren's office the day before and warned me that the walls were lined with golfing trophies. I played pretty well that day, and Caren beat me by ten strokes.

Bill Doan came to Indianapolis on several occasions. He was a likable person with a disarming charm. In an effort to satisfy DuPont that my company had nothing to hide and that our products would not harm their fibers, I opened up our entire operation to Bill Doan. He and Cy Gantt attended our school. We told him everything, including a few trade secrets.

Cy joined IICUC as a consultant when he retired. You can imagine my concern when Doan left DuPont and went to work for Steamway, a competitor. After Doan joined Steamway, we noticed a shift in their strategy, which even included a referral network similar to our Operation ABC.

The Masterseries Caper

Perhaps the greatest challenge to our chemical business came in the late '80s when seven chemical suppliers formed a cartel and tried to effectively freeze Bane-Clene out of the loop with fiber producers and the rest of the industry.

Known as the "Magnificent Seven," they had the blessing of DuPont to manufacture stain blocker products which would be offered for sale to the consumer by professional cleaners. The elite group of chemical manufacturers were given the power to train professional cleaners in the use of the

Masterseries program and subsequent exclusive licensing by DuPont. The seven manufacturers were even given access to some of the stain-resist technology.

Trade magazines were emblazoned with ads touting the sales potential of this after-market miracle product. Masterseries would restore stain-resistant qualities to fifth generation carpet fibers. In fact, this new line of products could even be used on wool and old nylon fibers which were not originally stain-resistant.

A few months after the introduction of Masterseries, DuPont decided to let us into the program. A class was offered at our school and applications were forwarded to DuPont, along with a $5.00 registration fee, which was a requirement of the program. We even put the products in our catalog.

Needless to say, we were offended and hurt that we were not originally asked by the DuPont Company to participate. The entire program was the biggest event in the history of the industry as far as a new product introduction was concerned. The Magnificent Seven and the DuPont Company spent huge sums on advertising to promote Masterseries.

With all of the hoopla, Masterseries was the biggest flop of the century. We were extremely fortunate that parochial interests tried to keep us out. Had we been asked to participate early, we would have put our money into the failed marketing program along with all of the other participants.

Naming Products

Most of our chemical products have a generic simplicity to their names. Initials such as "LCA" mean "Liquid Cleaning Agent." "OCC" translates to "Odor Control Concentrate." "TLS" stands for "Traffic Lane Spotter," and so on. Other federally registered trade names, such as "Emulon," were created in our laboratory.

Incidentally, a question I am often asked is "How did you choose the name 'Sta-Clene Formula 940'? Were there 939 other formulations before the final version?" Actually, "940" was the address of Elizabeth's residence in Philadelphia. I also remember her phone number. It was "POPlar 5-7384." I tend to be a little sentimental at times, so if you someday see a product named "7384," you'll know the origin.

XI

Bane-Clene Institute

Training People

My grade school and high school teachers were the most dedicated people I have seen in my lifetime. Articulate in their speech, their pronunciation and enunciation were perfect. I truly believe that my years under their tutelage was the equivalent of, or better than, a college degree by today's standards. Since that time, my experience with training programs, or lack of them, has made me a stickler for teaching people about the business.

In the Marine Corps, my teachers in the combat training units were all experienced combat veterans. Under the direction of Colonel Lewis B. "Chesty" Puller, their mission was to teach people how to survive, and they did a great job. From there on in the Marine Corps, training was not that good.

For example, I was transferred to a motor transport company at the Depot of Supplies on Schuylkill Avenue in Philadelphia at the end of World War II. Master Sergeant Pat Gallagher, the truck master, assigned me to drive a truck. I told him I had never driven a big rig and he said, "That's all right, kid. We'll teach you.

A big KR-10 International road tractor was assigned to me. Corporal Denny Ford, another driver, drove around the block with me to show me how to shift gears and hook onto a trailer. He really wasn't that good because, just about a block up Bainbridge Street, we dropped the trailer in the middle of the streetcar tracks. It was embarrassing trying to crank down the dolly wheels on the trailer so we could hook on again.

If it hadn't been for Harry North and Don "Paddy" Sharples, I would never have made it. Both of these men were Guadalcanal veterans and must have felt sorry for me. They took me under their wings, showed me how to back the rig up, and a few important things about driving on the road. From then on, I was on my own.

The big truck that bent in the middle

My first over-the-road trip was to New York City, with destinations at 90 Church Street in Manhattan, the Brooklyn Navy Yard, Floyd Bennett Field, and the U.S. Maritime Academy in the Bronx. I had never driven a truck that bent in the middle, much less tried to survive in New York traffic. Just finding my way to New York and back was an accomplishment. Amazingly, I came back in one piece and so did the tractor-trailer unit.

Gaseteria was better at training. A veteran driver took a new employee with him, taught the best routes and the intricacies and dangers of loading, hauling and off-loading gasoline.

At Brink's, I guess they took it for granted that I knew how to handle firearms. My first day on the job, Jimmy Ayres, the dispatcher, handed me a .38 caliber Smith & Wesson

Don "Paddy" Sharples (right) and me in Philadelphia.

revolver, a gun belt, and twelve rounds of ammunition. I had never handled a revolver. In the Corps I carried a .45 caliber pistol which was clip fed. I watched another man load a Colt .38 and quickly discovered that the S&W didn't release the cylinder the same way as the Colt. Apparently no one noticed that I was awkward in handling the piece. I carried that weapon nearly a year before I was asked to go to the police firing range to qualify.

No one at Brink's told me how to look for trouble. Everything, including bad habits, were picked up on the job from

*Photograph taken just before I left Brink's
to become a full-time employee of my son's company.*

people who were already there. Some of the truck employees were terribly careless, but no one in management did any sort of training, at least not at the Indianapolis branch office.

Training Carpet Cleaners

Training people how to use and maintain our equipment has always been a matter of principle with me. My own lack of training remains fresh in my mind. Trying to learn to clean carpets was extremely frustrating. It seemed as though no one did any training. In the early '60s, we bought several carpet cleaning machines, but no one offered a training program.

Most equipment was sold by janitorial supply stores, and the salespeople had no interest in demonstrating how to use it after the sale was made. Manufacturers didn't have toll-free numbers in those days. When we went into the equipment supply business, I made up my mind that we would train people and make ourselves readily accessible in case of a problem.

Early training classes were easy for us. New owners were few, so when they came to town, we simply took them out on one of our trucks to learn all about the business. Wives would spend the time with Elizabeth, listening in on phone calls and learning how to process paper work. Unsophisticated as this sounds, it was a good way to learn about the equipment and the business in general.

As sales increased in the mid-seventies, the practice of training people in our customers' homes became cumbersome and sometimes offensive to our service clientele. Walter Griese, the ServiceMaster representative to whom I referred earlier, was not the only problem. Customers did not like anyone learning on their carpets and furniture. For this reason, we established a three-day class, complete with a written examination.

The classes were expanded to four-day, and finally to five-day sessions as the amount of information needing to be discussed kept increasing. Our classroom has been expanded over the years to seat sixty students and is equipped with audio/visual equipment. Classes are held monthly in Indianapolis and periodically at various locations throughout the country.

The Curriculum

I believe that teaching with discipline and absolute authority is the quickest and best way to impart knowledge. The lessons I learned in boot camp in the Marines have stayed with me all of these many years. I still can recite my serial number, my rifle number, the nomenclature of the M1 rifle, my general orders and many other things that were required. However, the methods by which they were taught would not be acceptable today.

Every man who spent time on Parris Island dreaded the insidious sand fleas. As we stood at attention they would bite and draw blood. One morning a man in formation slapped one, and Platoon Sergeant Jessie Proctor, the drill instructor, screamed, "Murderer! Who killed that sand flea?" When no one 'fessed up, he ordered every man in the platoon to dig a six-foot-deep hole and look for the dead sand flea so we could give it a decent burial. After that incident, no one ever slapped a sand flea again. Discipline and fear overcame the small inconvenience of being bitten by a sand flea.

Placing hands in pockets was absolutely forbidden. A man named Dalby, from Black Earth, Wisconsin, was caught with his hands in his pockets. For the next week, Dalby wore dungarees with the pockets sewn shut. Each pocket contained about ten pounds of sand. I don't recall ever seeing anyone with his hands in his pockets after that.

Personal hygiene was important in the Corps. The close quarters and raunchy conditions dictated taking showers whenever possible. One of the recruits in our platoon (I can't recall his name) was prone to skip his shower. Sgt. Proctor got down wind of him one day. That night he was taken to the beach, and every man in his squad gave him a sand bath in the surf. The floor brushes they used to scrub him brought blood to the surface of his skin, and he was raw for the next two weeks.

We had the sweetest smelling platoon in the Marine Corps after that.

A typical group of students at Bune-Clene Institute.

The Four A's

There certainly is no Marine Corps-style discipline at Bane-Clene Institute. But classes are fully supervised and students are graded on the four A's : Attention, Attendance, Attitude and Ability. And yes, there is a certain amount of discipline necessary in order to achieve certification.

Anything that is difficult to achieve is cherished, and students who normally lead active lives are corralled in a classroom for five long days. Determination and perseverance are definitely requirements for our school.

The Instructors

Twelve instructors with experience totaling 166 years in the cleaning business are involved in the week-long educational session. Management, advertising and operational experts conduct the classes. No other school in the industry offers the depth of experience or comes close to matching the quality of the curriculum at Bane-Clene Institute.

Company Certification

Certification is a buzz word in the cleaning industry. Ever since the introduction of stain-resistant fibers, carpet cleaners have been scrambling to become certified. Bane-Clene Institute has been training and certifying owners, managers and operators since 1978, eight years before Stainmaster carpets were introduced. Company certification is achieved when the management of a cleaning firm becomes certified at the school and then administers a video-based certification program to all employees of the firm.

Frustration

Our service company is a model operation. Its success has been achieved through trial and error in advertising and operations. One of the classes I teach is about advertising. As I address the students each month, I wonder who will listen to what I have to say and who will go out and make serious mistakes.

Occasionally I talk with someone who is having trouble getting business and invariably find that this person is not doing what has been taught in my advertising class. This is very frustrating to me. Every student is given a proven formula for success, free of charge. Why some use it and some don't is beyond my comprehension.

Sometimes I catch myself wishing I could use some of the techniques Jesse Proctor used in shaping up our platoon in boot camp.

XII

Working for Big Companies

L. S. Ayres & Co.

At the 1971 Flower and Patio Show in Indianapolis, an executive with L. S. Ayres & Co., a major department store, stopped by our booth and talked with Elizabeth about our new method for cleaning carpets. He asked her to call Salvatore R. (Sol) Petruzzi, who was Ayres' Director of Customer Service. Sol was interested in cleaning services and had a contractor providing service to his customers. He liked our method, and the next year we signed a contract to operate a licensed department

Salvatore R. (Sol) Petruzzi

for his store. Being in the right place at the right time resulted in a twenty-year association that grossed millions of dollars for our company. But more importantly, we learned a lot about customer satisfaction from Sol. He was a great inspiration, offered many good ideas about improving service to customers, and helped lend credibility to our growing supply business.

Sol attended many of our conventions and shared his expertise with everyone. His unselfish nature helped provide the entree for many Bane-Clene operators to major department stores in their own market area.

Operating a licensed department for a department store was a great learning experience. A licensed department is like a franchise, and we paid a percentage of our gross sales to the store. All advertising and operating expenses were borne by our company.

Ayres was a hundred-year-old family-owned and operated business with twelve stores in Indiana. It had been Elizabeth's favorite place to shop since we moved to Indianapolis in 1948. If she bought something at Ayres and wished to return it, the store would take the item back without question. The first rule was that the customer had to be pleased.

Ayres was a model department store in a time when that industry was the epitome of customer satisfaction. As an example, on our second Christmas in Indianapolis, we bought a shiny red wagon for Billy and asked for it to be delivered on Christmas Eve. We saw an Ayres' truck park down the street about a half block away. As we watched to see if the truck would stop at our house, the delivery man walked all the way up the street to see if the "coast was clear" to make the delivery. We told him Billy was asleep, and he walked back down the block, got the wagon and carried it back, fearing the truck would wake

*The little red wagon that the Ayres employee
so carefully delivered.*

the child. Ayres' employees were outstanding, and acts like these were the reason Ayres had such a great reputation.

Sol Petruzzi liked our philosophies about customer satisfaction. They were nearly identical to those of his store. The customer had to be satisfied. When we expanded into the residential carpet cleaning market in 1969, Elizabeth laid down the rules as if they had come from an Ayres' employee handbook. She admired the store, its personnel and policies and said our company would operate the same way.

We developed a sign frame for our trucks so Ayres' name would be seen as we arrived at a customer's home. When we worked for one of our own clients, our name would appear in the sign frame. I got the idea from watching a spy movie in

Ayres was located at the corner of Washington and Meridian in downtown Indianapolis for more than one hundred years.

which license plates were switched on an automobile. This allowed us the luxury of scheduling our trucks in one section of the city and changing signs instead of changing trucks to service the clientele of the various stores for which we worked in the course of a day.

We answered separate telephone lines, "Thank you for calling L. S. Ayres!" Ayres' invoices were used and their charge card was accepted. For all practical purposes, we were L. S. Ayres & Co. This same system was used for other department stores, dry cleaners and carpet sales outlets. At one point in time we worked under the name of twelve different companies in the Indianapolis area.

One time a local newspaper, *The Indianapolis News*, published a story under a headline, "Did You Notice?" A reporter had seen one of our trucks stop on a residential street, take the Bane name out of the sign frame and turn it over to display Ayres' name on the other side of the sign. The sign frame would hold three large metal sheets which were printed on both sides. The reporter mentioned that there was the name of Lazarus, another department store, on a sign underneath.

For several years, we operated a furniture cleaning plant at Ayres' warehouse. This was an extremely profitable

operation in which as many as one hundred pieces of furniture would be processed in a day. Ayres' trucks picked up and delivered the furniture. Unfortunately for us, they closed the warehouse operation.

Ayres was purchased by Associated Dry Goods in the mid '70s, and we survived that buy out, but in 1991 ADG sold out to the May Company. Our contract was terminated in 1992 after twenty years of service. It is interesting that executives and former owners of the company still call us to clean for them even though the May Company has a new contractor.

Incidentally, Sol Petruzzi is one of the people who always encouraged me to write a book.

Lazarus

For a few years we worked for Lazarus, another major Indianapolis department store. A comedy of errors developed in 1979. Furniture to be cleaned for a Lazarus customer was taken to our plant in Ayres' giant warehouse facility. In fact, Ayres' trucks picked up and delivered furniture for Bane customers as well as Lazarus customers.

A Lazarus customer called to question why his sofa had been picked up by an Ayres truck. We explained that Lazarus did not have a pickup or delivery service. We had Lazarus' permission to do this, and it seemed to satisfy him.

In cleaning the sofa, an unusual problem occurred. The material was Haitian cotton and the white sofa turned brown. This was before we knew all there was to know about this particular problem, and we began a slow process of correcting the matter. It required a telephone call to the Lazarus customer to explain that the piece would not be returned when promised.

The browning was so severe that the piece was trans-ferred from Ayres' warehouse plant to our own plant on Keystone Avenue, where special attention could be given the problem. A week went by and our people were making headway, but we were not sure the solution to the problem would satisfy the customer. We called to describe our progress, and he offered to come to our plant to see if the work was satisfactory before we proceeded further. Otherwise, we were prepared to replace the piece of furniture at our expense.

The Lazarus customer who had his furniture picked up by an Ayres' truck now walked into Bane-Clene's plant to inspect the sofa. Even though he was a little bewildered, he agreed that the work done so far was satisfactory and that we should proceed to do the entire piece. He demanded, however, that it be returned on the next Saturday when he would be at home to inspect the piece.

Ayres' trucks delivered on Tuesday, Thursday and Saturday south of the center of the city and on Monday, Wednesday and Friday on the north side. The Lazarus customer happened to live north. Fearing any further unhappiness to be wished upon him, we decided to deliver the piece ourselves, but on that particular day the only furniture van we had was away from the city.

All of the empty vans we had for equipment installation were gone or had the tanks and equipment already installed . . . except for some that had Sears' decals. At the time we were outfitting trucks for Sears' Cleaning Service. A Sears truck was commandeered in the emergency and dispatched with orders to park around the corner from the Lazarus customer's house.

As our men pulled up to park, the Lazarus customer came around the corner with his poodle on a leash and stopped dead in his tracks when he saw his sofa being unloaded from a Sears truck. Inside his home, as the plastic wrapping was being removed, he said, "Don't say anything. I'm so confused now I don't want to talk about it." As our men left, they said he was standing on his porch shaking his head in disbelief.

A few years later, Lazarus' officials terminated our contract because of a disagreement about the amount of money they would receive. We operated at Ayres with 10 percent of our gross sales going to the store. That arrangement allowed us to stay competitive in pricing, meet our expenses and make about a 10 percent profit. Lazarus took 30 percent, which put us in a precarious pricing position. The separation was amicable. We just couldn't get together on price.

Five years after Lazarus terminated our contract, we were approached again to see if we had changed our minds. Once again in 1995, we were contacted by Lazarus to do their work in Indianapolis.

We never got together again.

Sears

We go back a long way with Sears. In the mid '70s, Robert G. McCaffrey of Philadelphia signed an agreement with Sears to operate carpet cleaning services in Sears' name anywhere East of the Mississippi river.

In 1978, Chrommaloy Industries in St. Louis signed a similar contract with Sears for the territory West of the Mississippi River. Both companies had permission to go just about anywhere they wanted to operate under Sears' name.

In 1979, Chrommaloy purchased fifteen Bane-Clene truck-mounted units, and RGM ordered 106 truck-mounted systems from us. To give you some idea of the scope of Sears' operation, they had over five hundred contractors nationwide. We dealt with only ten of them, including Chrommaloy and RGM.

Sears Cleaning Service trucks at Indianapolis Bane-Clene plant.

In 1980, Harry Stecker, Bob McCaffrey's Vice-President, called me to demand a lower price on our equipment. I told him we couldn't do it. Harry had been hired by RGM from Sears and had a vast knowledge of the workings of that company. He was an abrupt man who used heavy-handed tactics to get his way. Shortly after that, RGM was sold to Keystone Foods, a restaurant supplier.

Keystone Foods had the capability of building stainless steel products and started supplying the carpet cleaning operation with their own equipment. That firm was then sold to Northern Foods, Ltd., of Hull, Yorkshire, England.

I was relieved when Sears Cleaning Services stopped doing business with us. They had a way of taking us away from our bread-and-butter customers. Mike Wheatley of Virginia Beach, Virginia, was a good Bane-Clene customer. Mike operated several trucks under Sears' name and was displaced by RGM when they decided they wanted the Virginia Beach territory. The same thing happened to several others who had contracts with Sears. I always felt that these customers resented the fact that we sold equipment to RGM and Chrommaloy.

This was a pivotal time in our business, which I will discuss in more detail later. But, our business did increase in the four years after Sears stopped using our equipment. Part of it may have been due to the fact that there was some resentment in the cleaning industry toward anyone who did business with Sears. Several of my long-time customers who had expressed concern about our selling to Sears were relieved when they found out that we no longer did business with "The Giant."

They Just Didn't Understand

I was never able to convince anyone in the department store business that selling a service is not like merchandising hard goods. A service is intangible. It isn't there yet and cannot be produced until after the order is taken, and then it can only be built one at a time. Service can't be mass produced, stored in a warehouse and put on sale periodically.

Fine merchandisers that they were, department store people never understood that.

Amoco Fabrics and Fibers

One of the largest undertakings in which I have ever been involved took place when Don Barrett, Jr., asked us to take part in a large promotion by Amoco. Don was mentioned earlier as the son of a carpet retailer from Connersville, Indiana.

In 1988 Don was an executive with Amoco. He asked us to have Bane-Clene system owners throughout the country perform live demonstrations of a new Amoco product. During the next few years, members of Operation ABC did hundreds of demonstrations for Amoco in every section of the country.

Don gave us a list of cities and dates on which he wished to have a demonstration, and my office would arrange for someone to be there. I didn't see an actual demonstration until we had been doing them for about six months, and I must say, I was shocked. Amoco's "rollout" of the new Marquesa Lana brand carpets came to Indianapolis, and I went to see the demonstration at the Radisson Plaza Hotel.

Dan Cochran, who was in charge of this particular event, invited everyone in the audience to come up and deposit all sorts of things on this poor carpet. Mustard, ketchup, coffee, bleach, shoe polish, battery acid . . . you name it, and it was put on the carpet.

Then Dan asked our company representative to come forward and clean the carpet sample. Don Barrett has a favorite expression. He says, "A presentation without a demonstration is just conversation." This was a wild demonstration. I've got to admit that I was not sure those horrible stains would come out and even less certain how the carpet would look after the experiment.

The carpet sample came through with flying colors. In fact, the texture and color of the sample were not altered, which

Many, including me, gasped when the audience poured mustard, shoe polish, battery acid, and bleach on the carpet.

surprised me. The development of Marquesa Lana was one of the major advances in carpet technology, and I was extremely honored to be a part of it. Later, Amoco introduced another product called Genesis and did the same type of demonstration for carpet retailers, carpet specifiers, architects and mill representatives.

Shaw Industries bought Amoco's Olefin extrusion plant after Amoco's corporate headquarters decided to get out of the fibers business.

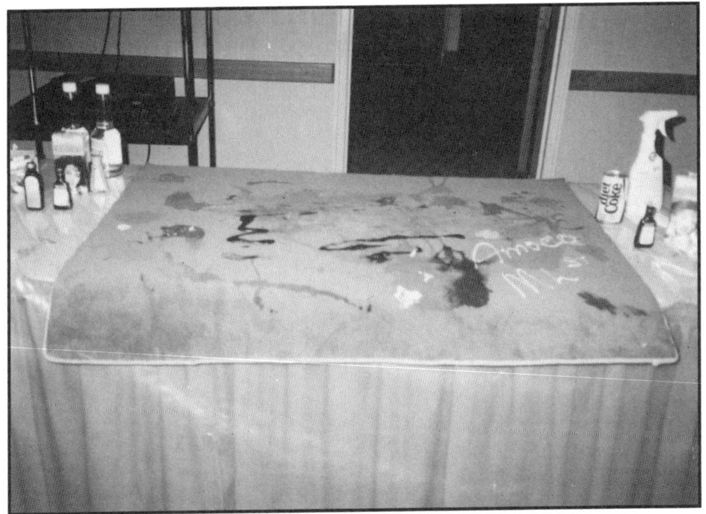

This was how the carpet looked after the audience finished.

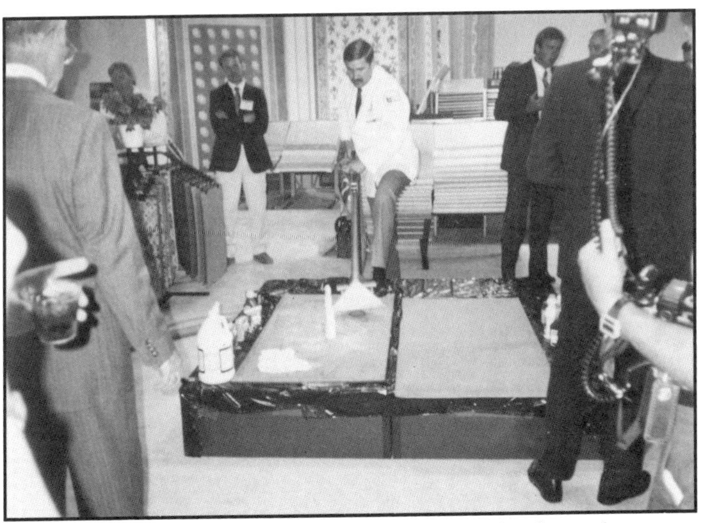

Kevin Stark prepares to clean the mess made by the audience at the Amoco Marquese Lana/Genesis "rollout" in Indianapolis.

Hercules Company

The famous fiber brand which produced some of the most popular furniture in history went into the carpet fiber business on the heels of Amoco's success. Ann Marquardt, who was headquartered in Norcross, Georgia, arranged for Bane-Clene operators to do a demonstration similar to the one we did for Amoco.

The Hercules demonstration was not nearly as flamboyant as Don Barrett's; however, the demonstrators did a good job in promoting a new product called Nouvelle. That program was halted abruptly when DuPont purchased the production of all the polypropylene products for the next five years from Hercules.

Abbey Carpets

In 1992, Jonathan Trivers, President of Abbey Carpets, expressed an interest in establishing a carpet cleaning division. Steve Bradley, an Abbey dealer in Watertown, New York, had purchased Bane-Clene equipment and was doing well in the business. Abbey is a franchise operation, with more than five hundred stores throughout the nation.

Jon Trivers and Phil Gutierrez, Chairman of Abbey Carpets, were extremely interested in the well-being of their franchisees. They wanted nothing from us in the way of remuneration for the privilege of doing business with their people. In fact, we were asked to pass any volume savings along to the individual franchisee.

Abbey people are of high caliber, and the relationship has been one of great satisfaction for all parties. Abbey's interest was only in becoming a full-service facility so they could maintain the products they sell and install.

Abbey dealers show off their new Bane-Clene carpet cleaning equipment after attending school in Indianapolis.

Shaw Industries

The first time we heard from Shaw Industries, we nearly went into shock. Shaw produces about a third of all of the carpet that is manufactured throughout the world, and the fact that they wanted to come to our school in Indianapolis made everyone in the company extremely nervous. We gave the best presentation we could, and the folks from Shaw came back on several occasions and called many times.

Carey Mitchell, the Director of Technical Services at

Carey Mitchell, Director of Technical Services for Shaw Industries, spoke at the 1991 and 1996 conventions.

Shaw, made several trips to Indianapolis. He is a quiet man who would make an excellent poker player. He never gave us much indication of how we stood with him. But we must have done well because Shaw Industries now recommend Bane-Clene in their maintenance brochures, which are distributed to the customers of the many brands they manufacture.

Joyce Lamb, Scott Wright, Cindy Sayre, Sam O'Brien and Ken Padgett have all spent time with us and have attended Bane-Clene Institute. Shaw Industries bought a Bane-Clene system for use in their state-of-the-art testing facility in Dalton, Georgia, and, without a doubt, has been a catalyst in the success of our company, especially Operation ABC.

Indiana Bell Telephone Company

In the mid '70s, Indiana Bell installed a quarter of million square feet of new carpeting in their downtown Indianapolis headquarters. It had a level loop nylon face fiber with a jute-on-jute backing system. It was glued directly to the concrete floor and the people who sold and installed the carpet told Indiana Bell officials never to wet-clean that particular carpet. Bell people were told that a steam cleaning method would cause shrinking, seam separation and delamination of the carpet backing system.

For more than a year, the Bell people followed that advice and used foams and powders in their maintenance program. The aesthetics deteriorated rapidly. Top management was becoming very dissatisfied with the appearance of the carpeting. Spots were reappearing quickly, and the entire building was taking on a matted, dull look. Traffic lanes were very evident and the overall appearance of the carpet was marbleized.

Our theory about the managers and owners of big buildings living someplace else proved to be true. The vice president who was in charge of all of the buildings and grounds owned and operated by Indiana Bell took his troubles home with him one evening, as so many of us do. Listening to his complaints, his wife asked, "Why don't you use the people I use to clean our carpets?"

The next morning, I got a call from Joe Wagner, who was the building superintendent, and we met to discuss the matter. That led to one of the best jobs we've ever had. We stationed equipment at the building and each evening dispatched a technician to work there between 5:00 p.m. and midnight. Special attention was given to high traffic areas every night. The carpet was always dry by the time people came to work the next morning. This building became a showplace and testimonial to the fact that proper maintenance solves major problems.

The job lasted until Ameritech took over the company and decreed that the carpet cleaning operation must be part of a janitorial contract. The janitorial company bought Bane-Clene equipment, and we trained them to do it right, but we still miss that job.

Maintaining the carpeting for Indiana Bell during those years was one of our proudest achievements, especially since they had been told that our method would not be good for the carpet.

Awesome Experience

Representatives of two of the largest janitorial firms in Washington, D.C., came to visit us during 1973. Chuck Hudson and Jerry Mirock were vice presidents of large companies that employed more than a thousand people, and we wondered why they would come to us for information. The answer was that their people didn't know how to clean a carpet. Hudson and Mirock were intrigued by a mailer we sent them.

We were concerned that a little Mom and Pop operation such as ours would seem hokey to them, especially since we had only been in the carpet cleaning business a few years. Both men were extremely polite and respectful. They asked good questions and wanted to see the work being done. We tried our best to impress them and to show what we do and how we do it.

Most of our work was residential, but we knew Hudson and Mirock were interested in looking at commercial jobs. While showing them both residential and commercial work, we were surprised that they seemed more interested in the residential locations where we demonstrated our equipment and techniques.

The answer came when both men resigned from their large companies and went into the residential cleaning service. Chuck Hudson did it right away and became very active during the next few years in the resolution of the great steam controversy. Jerry made the move several years later.

There is something special about operating a small business.

XIII

Advertising

It's Like Fishing!

Ever since we began looking for clients in 1962, I have enjoyed advertising tremendously. It is fun mailing out something to someone I don't know and getting a call in return. I guess it is very much like fishing, and there is a certain rush or thrill when you get a nibble.

The office cleaning business didn't require much in the way of advertising. But the consumer-oriented carpet cleaning venture depended on advertising to reach the targeted market. Advertising and sales promotion have been the main thrust of my efforts in our company since 1969.

Early advertising for our service company was mostly by direct mail. In 1976, I hired McGrath & Co., an Indianapolis advertising agency, to give our operation some professional polish.

The agency would place ads, and in addition to a retainer, fees included a 15 percent commission for space they purchased and for production costs. We did newspaper advertising, radio and some television to augment our Yellow Pages program during the years we used the agency.

Our Own Ad Agency

Advertising people knew nothing about our business, and I wound up writing most of the copy, so we terminated the ad agency's contract in 1981. Media Associates, our own in-house advertising agency, was formed and now operates as a division of our company. The name was suggested by Lee Holst, who was with the Yellow Pages Division of Indiana Bell at the time. Lee is a family friend and before he retired, lectured for years to the advertising class at Bane-Clene Institute about the benefits of Yellow Pages advertising.

Working directly with printers and other vendors and having our own creative staff has been a tremendous advantage and has given us a competitive edge, not only in our local market, but nationally and internationally, as well.

Media Associates has proven to be a major asset for those people who use Bane-Clene systems. Designing and using brochures, tapes and scripts for our service company and then customizing them for Bane-Clene owners passes along the economies of mass production. Owners may purchase a few hundred brochures for a price per copy that would be available only to someone who purchased hundreds of thousands.

Full-color separation charges are spread over the entire run, and we are able to provide full-color, high-quality advertising material for less than someone would pay for one-color material produced at a quick-print shop.

Co-op Advertising

One of the major successes of Media Associates has been the ability to bring competitors together in a mutual advertising effort. For example, members of Operation ABC are sharing the cost of advertising in the Yellow Pages. If two companies go together on an ad, they automatically cut the cost in half. If three are involved, the cost is only a third.

This allows a small operation the luxury of being in a dominant position in the Yellow Pages while paying only a small part of what it would cost otherwise. Some people co-op radio and television commercials, too. The same principle applies.

Franchises are extremely successful because the participants pool their advertising resources. Our co-op program was established to give our entrepreneurs equal footing with Stanley Steemer, Chem-Dry, ServiceMaster and other aggressive franchises.

The Professional Cleaning Digest

Without a doubt, the greatest advertising accomplishment we have had is publishing *The Professional Cleaning Digest* magazine. It began as a simple one-sheet newsletter that we mailed to our equipment customers in 1970.

An old used ditto machine was purchased for fifty dollars. It printed in a faded purple color and the quality was terrible, but people seemed to like the newsletter. We would relate any successes we had in our service business, especially in advertising and sales promotion, along with tips about managing the business.

The newsletter was renamed in January of 1981 since the format had been changed to that of a magazine in the mid-seventies. Quality has been constantly improved over the years, and today the publication has thirty-two pages, printed on enamel paper with photographs in full color.

It wasn't always that way. Before the advent of the computer, Oka typed the *Digest* copy as many as twenty times before it was sent out for typesetting. Then, each time there was a change on a proof copy, she had to reread the entire piece to see if any other typesetting changes had been made by mistake.

Today, Mary Kay Matson is the editor of *The Cleaning Digest* and works on modern computer equipment. The entire publication is produced and proofed in our own office. Sport Graphics, Inc., of Indianapolis does the full-color printing. Jim Johnston, who has worked with us since 1982 on the printing of the magazine, retired in April of 1996. He helped make it the standard of the industry.

The Cleaning Digest is distributed regularly to our equipment and chemical customers throughout the world. It is sent to carpet manufacturers as a courtesy and also to prospects who have inquired about our method. In addition, "cold" mailings are sent periodically to others who may be interested in the carpet cleaning business.

Our regular mailing is about 22,000 for each issue. Mailings to special groups such as dry cleaners, carpet retailers or janitorial services often increase a single mailing to 50,000 magazines. *The Cleaning Digest* has the largest distribution of any trade publication in the cleaning industry.

In 1995, a collection of the best articles from *The Cleaning Digest* for the previous twenty five years were compiled. The book consists of 512 pages and is the nearest thing our industry has to a textbook.

Patents, Trademarks and Copyrights

In 1974 we began registering trademarks with the U.S. Patent Office. Slogans such as "Call 'Us' On the Carpet" were submitted to the patent office in Washington, D.C., along with the trade names of our products. It was 1976 when we registered our hose-bordered advertisement as a trademark. It is now used by members of Operation ABC in America as well as overseas.

Two federal patents were obtained: one is for the apparatus we developed, and the other is called a process patent. These were very costly to acquire, and it took several years to complete the legal work. But twice, we have been successful in stopping builders from duplicating our machinery.

Trademarks cost much less to register than patents and take about a year to process. Copyrights are the least expensive to register. Very early, it became apparent that our advertising material was being copied and used by competitors. Since that first experience, we have faithfully registered and copyrighted every bit of advertising material we have produced.

A grand old lawyer named Harold Woodard led our company through the legal hoops of registration. Hal was like the proverbial country doctor who could make you feel good just by talking with him.

Infringers

The first test of the value of registering our trademarks came in 1978 when Robert Grimaldi, of Springfield, Massachusetts, took liberties with our hose border design. Even though he had changed it substantially, we objected to his using it and asked him to stop. He refused, and eventually a suit was filed in U.S. District Court in Springfield, Massachusetts. Our position prevailed.

In 1987, a company named Big Red placed our material in a Yellow Pages ad in Nashville, Tennessee. The owner claimed that a Yellow Pages representative designed the ad for him. A civil action was filed in U.S. District Court in Nashville against Big Red, L. M. Berry & Co., and Bell South. Again, our position prevailed. In addition to a cash settlement, the Yellow Pages representative who had appropriated our material was fired.

Unfortunately, Big Red went out of business in the process.

Attempts to Plagiarize Our Patents

In June of 1992, we began getting calls from our equipment customers informing us that someone was advertising a machine which looked similar to ours. A sketch in a trade magazine did look like our equipment, and a photo in a later issue clinched it. The machine had even been painted blue to look as though it were a Bane-Clene unit.

The machines were being built by Hallmark Manufacturing Company in Alabama; the firm was owned by Gayle Hall. Doug's Sales and Service, owned by Douglas Daniels, was the distributor. Doug had a business in Northern Indiana. A suit was filed on January 25, 1993, in United States District Court in Fort Wayne, Indiana, naming Doug Daniels and Gayle Hall as defendants.

A consent decree and final judgment were issued by the judge on February 11, 1993, supporting Bane-Clene's position. Without a doubt, this was the swiftest justice ever dispensed in the legal trials and tribulations of dealing with people who have attempted to plagiarize our patented, registered and copyrighted material.

In 1994, a federal lawsuit was filed in Kalamazoo, Michigan. For more than three years, David Thomas had been warned not to use our material. Ameritech, the Yellow Pages publisher, was also asked not to use our federally copyrighted art work and phrases.

The law states that the owner of a copyright or trademark must pursue infringers or lose the rights to the material. Having no alternative, a suit was filed against Mr. Thomas and Ameritech Publishing Company. With the precedents in the federal court system from our previous litigation, this suit took less than a year to resolve. Once again, our position prevailed.

An injunction was granted by the court, and a cash settlement, paid by Ameritech and Mr. Thomas' insurance company, was awarded to Bane-Clene.

We have persistently pursued copyright and trademark infringers. More than four hundred registered letters are mailed each year to people who, perhaps unknowingly, use our material. Nearly all discontinue once they are notified of the infringement. The others are contacted by our lawyers.

It has never been our intention to harm anyone through legal action. Over the years we have invested a small fortune in advertising, and now Bane-Clene owners, who are licensed to use the material, are spending millions of dollars each year placing our advertising throughout the nation.

We have a strong obligation to protect their investment as well as our own.

XIV

Saturday's Children

The Company of Firsts

In the late '70s, our company became known in the industry as the "company of firsts" because of an interview I did with *Indiana Business & Industry* magazine. Ann Hughes, the editor, asked me, "How do you come up with all the new ideas you have introduced to the cleaning industry?" I told her it was simply because we are IN the service business. Every development in equipment, chemicals and technique has been the result of our own experience.

Ann wrote a story entitled "Saturday's Children," which reflected many of the answers I gave her during our interview. "Your company seems to be unlike others in the business," she began. "What makes you so different?" I told her that most cleaning is done with the rotary method, dry foam, or powder, while we use external extraction and exhaust the recovered water and air outside the building. This interview with Ann Hughes took place many years before the concern over indoor air quality. Our system was enhancing indoor air quality long before it became popular to do so.

The main thrust of her article, however, was the fact that she interviewed me on Saturday morning. Elizabeth and I were working, the phones were ringing, and the office was humming. We always worked on Saturday.

Whenever our family gets together, even for celebrations, we inevitably end up talking about business. It is our life, and we enjoy working together and talking about it. Some would look on this as a curse, but doing something that is mutually rewarding is the finest way a family can communicate. Business is the perfect vehicle and provides outstanding rewards.

Every success has a cost. Sometimes it's as simple as working on Saturday, or it might be giving up a vacation or foregoing a new car and, instead, investing time and money in the business. Each reward has a risk and a sacrifice attached.

Learning to balance these elements is the key to winning in business.

The Lucky Syndrome

Years ago, when we first started our business, Gene Edgecomb, a young employee, said, "You sure are lucky. I took in $200 more than my pay for the day, so you four Banes get $50 each. You sure are rich."

Obviously, our schools have ignored teaching the principles of being in business and the realities of overhead expenses and taxes. At the time, the four of us didn't even draw a paycheck because there was nothing left after we paid our employees and the bills.

One time, when a tree service was cleaning up after a terrible ice storm had wreaked havoc on the trees on my property, Rhoda Rossiter, a neighbor, said to me, "You're lucky you've got such a good business so you can pay for all of this."

The great Earl Nightingale, speaking at our 1977 convention and discussing luck, said, "The harder I work, the luckier I get." Luck has nothing to do with success, but in the modern lottery mentality, more and more people are sitting back waiting to win life's lottery instead of working hard to succeed.

Those who make the effort to attend school and work hard will find themselves among the "luckiest" people in the world. I really believe there is a power greater than all of us that determines our route to success and safe passage along the way . . . but it's not luck. It's called "being blessed."

Innovations

In 1973 we installed toll-free incoming WATS lines, primarily for servicing our new equipment and chemical customers. Radio dispatching was new to the industry when we installed the first radios in our service vehicles.

One of the major improvements we brought to the industry was perfecting the use of the heat exchanger principle to heat our cleaning solution. Lines are connected to the radiator hoses of the truck and the hot engine water is plumbed through coils in the solution tank.

The heat from the truck engine, which would otherwise be wasted, is used to heat the cleaning solution as we travel from job to job. An automatic valve shuts off the engine water at a desired temperature, and insulation holds the heat so that the engine does not have to be operating while the actual cleaning is taking place.

With the chemical in suspension in the large tank, the constant agitation assures a good working solution with as little chemical as possible. This innovation is probably the most significant of all because it makes us extremely competitive in the raw costs of doing business.

The World Wide Web

Another major innovation at Bane-Clene was taking a site on the World Wide Web in 1995:

http://www.iquest.net/bane/

If not the very first, we were among the first in our industry to become a part of this exciting new communications phenomenon.

Matthew, Lois and Billy's son, has assumed the responsibility of placing our catalog, spotting guides, trouble-shooting charts and even our magazine, *The Cleaning Digest*, on the internet system.

*The fleet had expanded considerably
when this photo was taken in 1982.*

Trailer-mounted system was new innovation to the industry.

Another innovation is the "Bane-Trane" for airports and large shopping facilities. As many as five trailers can be towed to cleaning locations.

XV

War Stories

"I Get No Respect!"

Rodney Dangerfield would have cringed from some of the treatment I have received over the years. For example, when ChemLawn decided to go into the carpet cleaning business, a vice-president from the franchise headquarters in Columbus, Ohio, came to see me. He had talked to many people in our company about the business.

He stopped by my office one day to let me know that he was not going to buy our equipment. But this wasn't enough. He seemed to want to insult me. Our marketing approach "sucked," said he. "Your equipment has some good points, but we have developed a sure-fire marketing plan and we're going to build our own clone of a direct drive system," he added.

The man was arrogant. I'm really sorry I don't remember his name, but he was such a pompous individual and so insulting, I threw his card away as soon as he left my office. In parting, he told me, "I really feel sorry for little service companies like yours. When we get all two hundred of our offices up and running in carpet cleaning, we're going to put all of you little guys out of business."

In ChemLawn's few frantic years in the business, the company was fined $50,000 in Connecticut for discharging dirty water into a stream. ChemLawn obviously "took a bath" in the equipment endeavor, also. They sold off all of their "clones" at fire sale prices and nearly put the company from whom they copied the equipment out of business when they dumped the clones on the used equipment market.

There is a big difference between spraying fertilizer on lawns and cleaning a carpet.

Have a Nice Day!

Mrs. Phillips was a customer of our service company in 1973. She called to complain that our technician had used her bathroom and broken a wall tile. I went out to see the damage, and sure enough, a small 4" x 4" wall tile, located three feet from the ceiling over the bathtub, had been cracked.

It was obvious that our man couldn't have done it unless he stood on a ladder, but Mrs. Phillips insisted that it happened while he was in the bathroom. The tile was rather old, and it took several weeks to locate a replacement piece.

Each day, Mrs. Phillips would call me and berate my company for taking so long to correct the damage to her house. At the end of each vitriolic conversation, she would always exclaim, "Have a nice day!" I have detested that saying ever since.

By the way, we have a rule in our company that employees are never to use a customer's bathroom facilities.

The Auld Sod

A call came in one day in early 1970 from a customer. "Mr. Bane," he asked, "would you mind stopping out to see me?" Since we didn't know one another socially and had just cleaned the carpet in his home, I knew there must be a problem.

The next day I went to the home of George and Gladys Jenkins to investigate. As I turned in the driveway, I saw a large brown spot on the beautiful green lawn. Before we installed auxiliary tanks in our trucks, we dumped the dirty water anywhere we could. This was a poor choice since Mr. Jenkins and his wife were retired school teachers, and their lawn was their primary interest. I tried to convince him that a little fertilizer, a little rain and a little time would heal the brown spot.

He was very nice and obviously concerned, so I decided to settle the problem by sodding the brown area. A landscape company did the work, and two weeks later Mr. Jenkins called me to come out again. It seemed that the patch of sod didn't match the rest of the lawn. We eventually had to apply new sod to an entire section of his yard.

The Cul de Sac

Not long after we started our residential carpet cleaning service, Elizabeth called me to the phone to talk to an irate client. The woman was so exercised she could barely speak. "Your men poured dirty water on my cul de sac," she screamed into the phone. "I've got company coming tomorrow, and they left this horrible mess in front of my home."

We got out to Mrs. Wesley Harrison's home in time to clean up the mess before her company arrived. Incidents such as this and that of Mr. Jenkin's sod were responsible for the extra-large holding tanks in our trucks. The Harrisons are still customers, but I never will forget how upset Mrs. Harrison was with our company.

No Way Is It Wet, Mrs. Harris

It was a beautiful, sunny Saturday morning when Elizabeth got a call from a customer we had serviced on Friday afternoon. Mrs. Harris, the wife of one of the principals of Paul Harris Stores, was an extremely influential citizen. She said her carpet was still wet. Elizabeth put her "on hold" and asked me about it. "No way," said I. "The carpet just feels cool to the touch since it's so clean. Tell her to take a brown paper bag and place it on the carpet. If there is any water it will show on the bag."

"Mrs. Harris said the carpet was wet, so it's wet," Elizabeth said.

"Tell her I'll be right over," I replied as I grabbed a brown paper towel and my car keys.

On arrival at Mrs. Harris' home, I was ushered to her daughter's bedroom. I couldn't wait to show her that the carpet just felt cool to the touch because it was so clean. I took the towel from my coat pocket, got down on one knee and, as I did, became aware of a wet sensation. I got up and sheepishly looked at my khaki trousers. The right knee was soaked.

After making my apologies and scheduling a crew to redo the carpet, I hurried back to the office. Pat Brady had been the lead technician on the Harris job and was not working that day. Pat's truck was parked behind the office. It was just as he had left it. I drove it around to the front, plugged it in and checked the vacuum. There was hardly any suction at all. The dump gate on his base unit was open about a quarter of the way, which meant the vacuum was not sufficient for proper recovery.

I had a long talk with Pat on Monday. And I learned never to say, "No way!"

Mystery Spots

Franklin, Indiana, is a small bedroom community about twenty-five miles south of Indianapolis. We cleaned the carpets in the home of Mrs. Townsend in 1974. The invoice was for $67.35, which was a nice job in those days.

About two weeks after the job was completed, Mrs. Townsend called to complain that spots were appearing on her carpet where she didn't have spots before. A crew was scheduled to reclean the areas. When they asked where the spots were, Mrs. Townsend replied, "Oh! You can only see them at night." The technician cleaned all of the carpets again, thinking that this would satisfy the customer.

Two weeks later, Mrs. Townsend called again. The complaint was the same. We cleaned the carpet again. A month passed, and I thought we were clear on the complaint. Then she called again. This time I sent someone out after dark so they could see the mysterious spots. The spots were still invisible, but we cleaned the carpets again.

Another month passed, but this time I wasn't being lulled into a feeling of false security. I would wait and see if she really was satisfied. Two months passed, and I began to feel a little more secure. Then it happened. She called again. This time, she said she couldn't see the spots, but all of her neighbors could see them and were making fun of her. I said, "Mrs. Townsend, if I send your money back, do you think those spots would go away?" "Oh, my, yes!" came the hasty reply.

Elizabeth wrote the check and we took it down to the main post office that night.

EAKS!

Her name matched our recollection of this customer. Out of the many thousands of people for whom we have worked, it's amazing how the few rip-off artists stand out in my mind. Mrs. Eaks lived in Greenfield, a suburb just east of Indianapolis.

She called to complain that our literature said the carpet would stay clean longer with our method, and it hadn't. I replied, "Not to worry! We stand behind our work."

A crew was scheduled to Mrs. Eaks' home and after the job was done, Kevin Stark made a report. He suggested that we ask more "fact-finding questions" when taking a complaint.

For example, Mrs. Eaks' carpet had been cleaned seven months prior to the complaint. She had four children and a large dog. There was no grass in the back yard, which resembled a sea of mud. We marked her record accordingly.

At the time, we had five different people answering the phones, so a memo was circulated suggesting care be exerted in similar cases.

About a year later, Mrs. Eaks scheduled an appointment as a customer of L. S. Ayres & Co. When she was asked if we had ever done work for her, she replied, "No." She obviously didn't know we were the same people she had ripped off. The person who scheduled the job had not been with us the year before and put her on the schedule as an Ayres' customer.

We did the job for Ayres, and sure enough, we got the same complaint, this time nearly nine months after the job was done. She called the complaint department at the downtown Ayres store. We recleaned her carpets in the interest of customer satisfaction and marked both Ayres and Bane records to try to avoid working for her in the future.

Eleven months later, Mrs. George Marshall made an appointment with Lazarus at her home on the north side of Indianapolis. We did Lazarus' work at the time. Kevin Stark happened to be on the crew and reported that Mrs. Marshall was indeed Mrs. Eaks, that she had remarried, had the same children and dog, and was not the least bit embarrassed when she saw him.

We were three-time losers.

The Wrong House

It was a warm spring day in 1974. Our gleaming white service truck turned the corner in a quiet residential neighborhood in Indianapolis, slowed to search for the right house number, and then pulled into the driveway of the neat suburban home.

One of the men went to the door, rang the bell and waited. "Good morning," he said to the teenager who answered. "Is your mother at home?"

"No," replied the youngster. "She'll be back in a little while."

"We're here to clean the carpets. May we come in?"

"Sure," responded the young lady.

The men set up to do the job, checked the rooms to be cleaned on the invoice and went to work. As they were reeling up their hoses after the job was finished, a car pulled into the driveway behind their truck. A lady got out and asked, "Who are you?"

"We're the carpet cleaners," they responded.

Retorted the lady, "I didn't order any carpet cleaning service."

The crew apologized sheepishly and left. The story had a happy ending. The occupant of the "wrong number" called the office to say what a fine job the men had done and offered to pay if we would send an invoice.

A memo went to all employees to please check the name and address carefully in the future.

Seven Hours' Work for $25

Elizabeth sent Billy and me to do a job one day in the spring of 1972 for Mrs. Snyder, who was an interior decorator. She had asked Elizabeth for a demonstration at her home and said that, if she liked it, she would recommend us to her clients. She did not hesitate to ask for a substantial discount. Elizabeth told her we would do her living room, two halls, dining room and three bedrooms for $25, which was a considerable discount.

When we were finished with the assigned work, Mrs. Snyder said she was very impressed and asked us to do her basement sewing room, the stairs leading down to it, and a room in her sister's house, which was next door. We didn't want to offend her in any way, but we did ask for an additional $15, and she said to go ahead. It took nearly two hours to do the sewing room alone. There must have been two thousand pins in the carpet and most of them had to be taken out by hand.

The whole job took us about seven hours, and when we got back to the office, in addition to the grief we took for being so long, we also were chastised for adding onto Mrs. Snyder's bill. She had already called to complain that we had changed her invoice and charged her more than Elizabeth had quoted.

In the interest of customer satisfaction, Elizabeth told her to pay just the original amount. But the part that really hurt was Mrs. Snyder's implication that we weren't very good at our job. "How long have those two men been with you?" she asked. To which Elizabeth replied, "Oh, quite awhile." She never did tell Mrs. Snyder who we were.

The Judge's Wife

In 1974, we received a complaint on a job we did for L.S. Ayres in Lafayette, Indiana, which is about sixty miles from Indianapolis. A crew was sent back to rectify the problem. Another complaint from the same customer brought another trip from a service crew. Each time, an area that had not been listed on the original invoice was said to have been skipped. We cleaned the other rooms at no charge. This was a big house, too. But, the third time was just too much. Instead of sending a regular crew, Donnie and I went on the complaint.

We were in uniform so she could not have known that we were principals in the company as we knocked on her door. When she let us in, she said, "I hope you two can get this job straightened out. I had the last two guys fired who were sent here." We did the extra work at no charge and diagrammed the home on the record so she wouldn't be able to rip us off again. That did end the problem.

Ironically, about a year later, her husband, a judge, was sent to prison for fencing stolen property in his courtroom.

Clean Apartments for Free

The first year we were in the carpet cleaning business, we got a call from Gerald Hoover, who asked if we would clean an apartment for him as a demonstration. He said that if he liked our work, we could clean all of his "move-outs."

We jumped at the chance.

One day I was on an estimate near Mr. Hoover's complex, and as I drove by, I saw a competitor's truck in front of one of his buildings. I happened to be going past the same building a few days later and there was another cleaner's truck parked in front. I waited and spoke with the technician, who informed me that he was demonstrating for Mr. Hoover.

It was an insidious scam, inviting free demonstrations from different companies every time he had someone move out.

There were more than a hundred cleaning firms in Indianapolis at the time. I don't know how many of them were taken in by this scheme.

Sure enough, about a year later, he called us again. He must have worked his way through all of the free demonstrations. This time he said he was thinking about using our service, but asked if we would mind demonstrating for his manager, who had not been there before.

Elizabeth thanked him for calling and said we just couldn't get to it. He offered to wait until we could and called back several times. I guess he finally got the message because he stopped calling.

We all felt as though someday justice will be served in cases like that of the judge's wife, Mrs. Snyder, Mr. Hoover, Mrs. Eaks, and Mrs. Phillips, but it might be in the hereafter.

Too Hot

The very first carpet we cleaned with our new truck-mounted system in 1969 was an Eastman Kodel polyester shag. The brand was advertised as having "fat, fat" fibers. Each tuft stood about an inch and half in height. The face yarns were densely packed, and it was a beautiful floor covering.

We used 180° water to clean it, and when we finished, we could walk anywhere around that room, look down and see jute smiling up at us. Those fat, fat fibers resembled little shriveled-up mop strands. They lay over on their sides and died right before our eyes. I never forgot that lesson about what hot water could do to certain fibers. The reason I never have forgotten is because Elizabeth still reminds me of it from time to time.

The carpet was in our family room.

Cleaned By Capture

In the mid '80s, I started getting calls from Milliken Carpet Mills. A woman named Pat (I don't remember her last name) called me every week for about three months. She asked a thousand questions about the service business. At first, I got pretty excited that Milliken was interested in the way we clean carpets. Much to my chagrin, I found that they were in the process of buying the Capture method from DuPont.

Pat was just picking my brain about the industry, and we paid for all of the phone calls on our "800" number.

Furniture Cleaning

Earlier, I mentioned the white Haitian cotton sofa that we had cleaned for the Lazarus customer and how it turned brown, but there were other notable experiences in furniture cleaning that caused me to make the following decree: "Don't clean any more furniture!"

Harry Rossiter worked with us in the early '60s. We had purchased a Von Schrader Furniture Deterger in 1964, and Harry learned to use it. He was a very careful person and extremely customer oriented. One day he was busy cleaning a white sofa, when all at once a big, reversed purple number "4" started to bleed through from the backing material. That was when we found out that furniture builders sometimes use indelible marking pens on the back of the fabric.

Diana Mason had an Early American print on her furniture of *Washington Crossing the Delaware.* When we cleaned it, the General got out of his boat and blended with the waters of the river. Ginny Hardy's sofa seat cushions shrank. We didn't know you weren't supposed to take the covers off cushions to clean them.

Ayres' customers were especially demanding. One little lady said we had ruined her green velvet chair because it looked lighter when we finished cleaning it. The nap of the velvet could be set in either direction. One way looked dark; the other way made it look light. She said it didn't look good either way and that it definitely didn't look like it did when she bought it at Ayres in 1922.

We bought her a new chair and took the old one home. We used that chair in training classes for years. It has been cleaned thousands of times by hundreds of people and still looks halfway decent.

Learning how to clean furniture was the most painful of all of our learning experiences. We bought a lot of furniture in our first few years in the business. That's when I said to quit. When we started using the extraction method, Donnie and Kevin began cleaning furniture, and Elizabeth didn't tell me. I'm really glad I didn't know about it, or I probably would have worried myself to death.

Len Lepak taught us how to dry clean furniture and thanks to Donnie and Kevin's perseverance, we learned how to steam clean where it was appropriate. Furniture cleaning eventually became very profitable for us.

Tuchman Cleaners

For more than two years, I called on Sid Tuchman, the owner of a chain of dry cleaning shops in Indianapolis. Sid had called us to his home in the early '70s when one of his children had spilled something on the carpet. He called back later to say how impressed he was with our new cleaning method.

After that, I tried to convince him that we could do carpet cleaning for his customers just as we did for Ayres. He had about forty stores in the Indianapolis area, a solid customer base, and a great reputation in the dry cleaning business.

During my visits to his office, I sold him on going into the business all right, but he bought four HydraMaster truck-mounts and set up shop on his own. I didn't mind that nearly as much as when he came out with television commercials and newspaper ads saying that his was the first truck-mounted operation in Indianapolis. That really hurt.

Apparently the business was not what he expected because he got out just about as fast as he got in. He never would return my calls, so I don't know the reason, although I have a pretty good idea.

Achtung!

He was from Frankfort, Germany, and didn't speak a word of English. My German vocabulary was limited to "Gesundheit." Karlheinz Scheiman came to visit us in 1977 and brought an interpreter with him whose name was Hildegard.

Coincidentally, we had recently cleaned the carpets in Hildegard's home while Karlheinz was her house guest. According to her, he got excited about seeing the crew at work and said he was interested in importing our equipment to his country.

For three days we met for more than eight hours each day. At one session, we were still talking at 2:00 a.m. in our home. Elizabeth excused herself and left the room. After Karlheinz and Hilly had left, I found Elizabeth asleep on a chair in our bedroom. She swears that she just had to close her eyes for a minute and never intended to fall asleep, but I think she had seen and heard enough by that time.

We had lunch and dinner together each day and chattered back and forth through Hildegard. I never saw any two human beings eat as much as those two, and I truly believe they had just found a soft touch to pick up the check.

We never heard from Karlheinz again.

Lots of Water

Whenever anyone would throw an objection into our equipment sales presentation, I worked vigorously to find a counterpoint that would put us in a dominant position over the competition. Bob Leonard, of Bloomington, Indiana, said, "There must be an awful lot of water in that machine."

Billy and I were demonstrating for him and his brother in 1971. I was so naive that I replied, "Yes sir! It holds twenty gallons." He proceeded to explain to me that he was referring to excessive price, not the amount of water the base unit held. I stammered around and tried to explain our price. I told him we built the machines one at a time and used the best material available. He bought the system anyway, saying he could see the value in spite of my bumbling explanation.

Over the years, we became more proficient in explaining the benefits of our system. One of the best methods we found was the Jack Webb/Joe Friday approach . . . "Just the facts, sir!" And we always told the truth!

The Leonards were the first sale Billy and I made outside the Indianapolis area. I remember how excited we were as we drove home from Bloomington and talked about the possibility of selling our equipment elsewhere in the State of Indiana. It's doubtful either of us dreamed that some day sales would be made in every State of the Union, The Philippines, Canada, Mexico, South Africa, South America, the Virgin Islands, the United Kingdom, Scandinavia, China, Japan, Germany, United Arab Emirates, Lebanon, and the Irish Free State.

Not Enough Water

An objection that we had never heard before came in 1977. A person from California called to say he was interested in our equipment, but he couldn't justify buying it because California was in the throes of a water shortage. "Before long we won't be able to get enough water to take a bath, much less clean carpets. We're on the verge of having rationing," he told us. The man feared that he wouldn't be able to fill the big tanks on our truck. I went to work on the problem immediately.

Tom Schubert is a water treatment engineer. He was retained to draft plans for a water recycling system and drew detailed schematics of a plant that would be capable of taking the recovered water from a five-truck operation, filtering, treating and having it ready to use the next day for cleaning.

We labeled the highly secret operation "Project R" and formally introduced it at our convention in Clearwater, Florida, in January of 1978. That same week, the State of California was deluged with rains the likes of which hadn't been seen in forty years. Needless to say, we never heard any more from the man in California. The plans, however, were included in our equipment manual so anyone could build a recycling system in the event of a water shortage anywhere. The flooding in California in January of 1995 reminded me of the time I introduced Project R.

Unfortunately, Project R came back to haunt us. The local Stanley Steemer operation in Indianapolis picked up on it. The Stanley Steemer folks told prospects who were comparison shopping that if they had Bane clean their carpets, they should ask for a time early in the day. They would go on to say that we used dirty water over and over.

In our own company, Project R became known as "Bane's Folly." But the plans are still good and they will work. Someday they may prove to be very valuable.

The Barth Experience

Without a doubt, the worst business decision I ever made was trading in our GMC motor coach on a Barth diesel coach. The GMC had served us well on the Mini-Clinics for seven years, but since General Motors was not building them anymore, I was worried about the availability of parts and started shopping for a new vehicle.

Barth said all the right things. A Detroit diesel engine, Allison transmission, Bendix brakes, Kohler generator...every component was a well-known brand. I always suspected that Barth must have bought "seconds" or otherwise defective parts because during the first year alone, there were 121 failures of components, including the Dana cruise control. Even the microwave oven and the ice maker broke down and had to be replaced.

The Allison transmission had to be replaced on the side of the road in Ohio. The Detroit engine provided one monstrous problem after another. The last two trips ended on the back of a wrecker. The Kohler generator was unquestionably the worst of all the bad components on the Barth. It finally had to be replaced with an Onan generator because it never made a trip without breaking down. In fact the whole electrical system was a nightmare.

In Tennessee, there is a mountain called Monteagle. When the good old Bendix brakes failed, I rode the Barth down that mountain on the Nashville side. Talk about a thrill a minute! Another time up in New England, the air parking brake failed and the coach rolled away from a filling station with Oka and Elizabeth on board.

Finally, I had enough and advertised the coach for sale in a flyer that was mailed to more than 700 RV dealers. I put a picture of the beast on the cover with a big lemon emblazoned over it. The caption read, "The Biggest Lemon on the Road." The flyer listed all the problems I had with the machine and what parts had been replaced. It was offered for $50,000 to the first taker. I got eighty-four calls on that brochure. Don't ever think negative advertising doesn't get attention!

Jim Elie, of Atlanta, Georgia bought the lemon sight unseen. When he came to Indianapolis, I told him it was a lemon and that he would have trouble with it. He assured me that he knew what he was doing and that he was a mechanic and knew how to fix anything. "Besides," he said, "You've replaced nearly everything on it." At the time, the coach was at Barth's factory in Milford, Indiana, where they had supposedly checked it out.

Jim picked it up there, got as far as Dalton on the way home from Milford, and had to be towed the rest of the way to Atlanta. A month later, he called me and said the coach had been struck by lightening.

I told him so.

A Government Handout

I have a basic belief that there is no such thing as a free lunch. Our society today is smitten with government handouts in everything from welfare to tax abatement for business. Tax abatement is as wrong as someone ripping off the welfare system.

When I got out of the Marines in 1948, I was entitled (I hate that word) to join "The 52/20 Club." Every veteran could sign up and draw $20 a week for fifty-two weeks. I never took any of it. I was entitled to a free education under the G.I. Bill. I never took advantage of that, either. A G.I. Loan was available for me to buy a house, but when I bought my first house, I did it on a conventional bank mortgage. Something in me always resisted the temptation to take something for which I had not worked.

In 1990 Bill Hudnut, the Mayor of Indianapolis, asked me to keep our plant at its present location when we needed to expand. The State of Indiana had established an enterprise zone there and offered tax incentives to anyone who would expand business in that area.

Against my better judgment, I agreed to do it, and it has been the worst nightmare of my business career. In initial meetings, the State offered 30 percent Indiana tax credit on the $700,000 cost of the land and the building expansion. I expected a $210,000 tax credit and 100 percent inventory tax abatement. However, the State "granted" a 7 percent tax credit and 79 percent inventory tax abatement. When any government agency says they want to help, get it in writing and have them sign it in blood! Even the government uses bait-and-switch tactics.

One thing that the application for tax abatement did guarantee was that we would receive regular visits from auditors of the Indiana Department of Revenue. These disruptive procedures take weeks and are extremely distracting to the management of the company.

Every year, we spend the majority of the money we are supposed to save on tax abatement for high-priced lawyers to make sure that we get the tax incentives. Accountants and lawyers love tax abatement.

If I had it to do over, I definitely wouldn't do it.

Bribes

On more than one occasion, my family has found itself in the position of being solicited for a bribe. Building managers, insurance company representatives, and people in government have been guilty of such acts.

Elizabeth established our company policy the first time we had such an experience. She said, "When they hold out their hand, shake it!"

XVI

Long Distance Management

The St. Petersburg Experiment

Tim Condron and Bill Yeadon lived in St. Petersburg, Florida. Bill Yeadon and my son, Billy, had gone to school together and stayed in touch after graduation. In 1977, we formed a partnership with Bill and Tim for a cleaning operation in St. Petersburg.

Tim was as enthusiastic as I have ever seen a person about going into the business. Bill was a hard worker. They made a good team because of Tim's determination and drive and Bill's public relations ability.

A direct mail campaign kicked off the new venture. Through our affiliation with Associated Dry Goods, who owned L. S. Ayres, we obtained a contract with Robinson's of Florida, one of the major department stores in St. Petersburg. We used the same arrangement as that of our Indianapolis operation and worked under the Robinson name as well as that of Bane-Clene of Florida.

Within two years, Bill and Tim were running a six-truck office. Bane-Clene's advertising expertise and contacts had propelled the St. Petersburg experiment into an instant success. Maybe too instant!

By 1981, Bill and Tim were subcontracting all of the work in the Tampa Bay area and were both doing other things. When I learned the direction the operation was going, I thought it best to close it down. Shutting it down was painful for all of

*The St. Pete fleet lines up in front of Robinson's store
at Tyrone Mall.*

us. Tim had another business interest. We offered Bill a job in Indianapolis, and he stayed with us for ten years.

I was always sorry the St. Petersburg experiment didn't work out.

Distributors

In the early '70s, we tried to organize distributors for our chemical products and equipment. Everyone wanted to be a distributor, but no one wanted to pay for any inventory. We signed on a few distributors, and they were a disaster.

One of our so-called distributors wanted to hold a Mini-Clinic. When the time came to do the demonstration of our equipment, he used Amway powder in the tank. To get gum off the carpet he used a freezing chemical, which we did not recommend. Both demonstrations were a flop. That was the end of his distributorship.

One time we got a complaint about our anti-foam product from a customer in Phoenix, Arizona. He said it separated and "looked funny." He also said it didn't work as well as the product he had bought directly from us. I asked him to send the product to us so we could analyze it. We found that the product had 20 percent more water in it than when it left our plant.

The "distributor" had taken a gallon from each five-gallon container and added water to fill it up. Every four containers meant an extra five gallons of liquid product. That ended our distributor program until the '80s.

The United Kingdom

Bob Kelly was an exuberant man with an odd British accent. He wasn't British at all but had picked up a modification to his speech from living there. He was an American in the cleaning business in England.

Bob had been to Philadelphia to attend a wedding and had the opportunity to see our equipment. His uncle, John Poehlman, owns Bane-Clene systems. Bob wanted the same equipment for his office cleaning firm back in England. Being an outgoing individual and sales oriented, he wanted to become a distributor for our products in the UK.

I told Bob we were not interested in distributing in the United Kingdom, or anywhere else outside of the United States, for that matter. That was in 1981. He persistently called me every week to ask about a distributorship.

Bob had two partners, Daryl Wong and Alan Gin, who were of Chinese extraction. They had emigrated from South Africa and had a business installing office equipment in London. All three partners showed up in Indianapolis to persuade us that we should use them as our distributor. How could we say "no"?

In July of 1982, KDA (Kelly, Daryl and Alan) Associates formally opened our distributorship in the UK. All three partners were dedicated and hard working. They launched the program with a "mail shot," as they called it. A series of Mini-Clinics was scheduled and Bob asked that I make the tour with them.

Elizabeth and I were treated like Lord and Lady Bane. Bob rented a Rolls Royce limousine, complete with chauffeur,

Looking on as Bill Bane signs the agreement are (l to r)
Darryl Wong, Bob Kelly, and Alan Gin.

to pick us up at Heathrow Airport. As the chauffeur held the door, a woman rushed up toward the car. She must have thought celebrities were arriving. When he closed the door, she put her nose on the glass, peered in at me, and exclaimed in a delightful cockney accent, "'Ell! 'E ayin't nobuddy!"

With that still ringing in our ears, we were whisked away to Brown's Hotel, a 400-year-old legend in the hostelry business. The Brown's Hotel experience was fabulous.

During that trip, we stayed a few days at Selfridges Hotel, which is attached to Selfridges department store in London. Living in a department store! Elizabeth thought she had died and gone to heaven. She got to experience the famous Harrod's department store on that trip, and it is unquestionably one of her favorite places to shop. Come to think of it, I have yet to find a shopping place that she did not like.

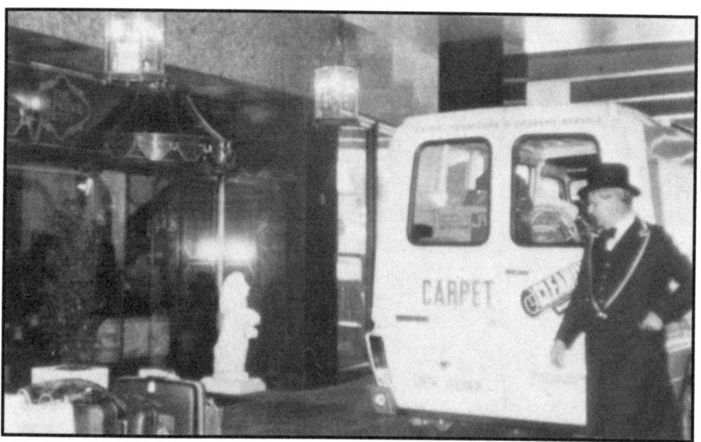

From a Rolls limousine at Brown's to a Renault carpet cleaning wagon at Selfridges Hotel! The doorman is skeptical.

During the next five years we made many trips to England and Scotland. I spoke to hundreds of people in the cleaning business in more than thirty cities. Those are pleasant memories, for the most part. One exception comes to mind. On my first trip, Bob Kelly told me, "Be careful not to use any

American slang. Things have a different meaning here than they do in the States."

Besides differences in language, English carpet cleaners were different from an American audience. Ours are more informal and dress casually. In England, they showed up in three-piece suits, carried brief cases and sat rigidly as though at attention. I was uncomfortable as I stood in front of them.

In America, I always tried to bring a little humor into my presentations. The audience did not seem to "get" any of my "funny" stories. Midway through my first presentation, I was talking about people in the business who used the shampoo method. In pointing out the difficulty in maneuvering the equipment, I used the example of a man "dragging a scrubber up the stairs." The audience almost fell out of their chairs laughing. After the meeting, I asked Bob what I had said that was so funny. I wanted to be sure to use it to loosen up the staid British audience at future meetings. Kelly said, "I don't think you want to say that again, Bill. In English slang, a 'scrubber' is a prostitute."

The Spurgeon Family

In 1984, George Spurgeon, his wife Joan, and her brother, Brian Banks, came from Crawley in Sussex to Indianapolis. They had become interested in our system; however, they were a little skeptical of some of the things Bob Kelly was telling them. They came to attend our school and make an assessment for themselves.

The family operated a successful Daily Office Cleaning business around Gatwick Airport and were interested in carpet cleaning. After a week at school, they returned to the UK, bought equipment from Kelly, and a year later, with our

L to R, George Spurgeon, Karen Lamb, The Right Honorable Nicholas Soames, Chris Spurgeon, Joan Spurgeon, and Brian Banks. The directors of Spurgeons Clean Plan Ltd. assist Mr. Soames in the ribbon-cutting ceremony at the dedication of the new facility in Crawley, England, on June 1, 1987.

wholehearted approval, purchased the distributorship from KDA.

Since that time, the Spurgeon firm has devoted a great deal of time and effort to promoting Bane-Clene Systems. They have opened a new warehouse and office facility for the distribution of our products and established a full-time school patterned after Bane-Clene Institute in Indianapolis. They operate Sparkle Clean, which is a carpet, upholstery and curtain (drapery) cleaning service.

The Spurgeons' son, Chris, and son-in-law, Rob Lamb, who had worked for British Airways, have joined the company. Chris' wife, Sue, and Rob's wife, Karen, both work in the business. Brian continues to oversee the DOC side of the company. This is truly a family business.

In 1987, Elizabeth, Oka and I went to Crawley for the dedication of Spurgeons' new building and had the honor of meeting Nicholas Soames, a member of Parliament who cut the ribbon during the ceremonies. Mr. Soames is the grandson of Sir Winston Churchill. I felt a sense of touching history when I shook hands with him.

During that visit, we had the opportunity to meet many of the Spurgeons' friends and see firsthand why they are so successful. Employees were treated with great respect, and the entire family worked hard and is extremely dedicated.

Sadly, Joan passed away in 1995. She was a great golfer, a regal lady, and earned admiration from everyone who knew her in her long battle with dreaded cancer.

Mr. Soames is presented by Bill Bane with a set of Bane-Clene commemorative coins.

First class in Las Vegas

Las Vegas Distribution Center

The distribution of our products to the West Coast has always been problematic. Freight charges kept us from making a profit and giving our customers prompt service. In 1993 we opened a distribution facility in Las Vegas to serve our West Coast customers. This center allowed us to have our products in the customers' hands overnight nearly everywhere on the Coast.

By shipping complete truckloads of chemicals and equipment, we cut freight costs dramatically, and our presence in Las Vegas has eliminated the only objection of West Coast people to doing business with us. Now, we're not very far away.

Joe and Susan Hill were transferred from Indianapolis to Las Vegas in June of 1993, and in July we opened up for business. Susan had worked in our service company as a telephone specialist, while Joe had been a customer service representative for Bane-Clene.

In March of 1995, we conducted our first school in Las Vegas and were totally surprised by the attendance. More than one hundred people registered, ninety-eight attended, ninety-one took the examination, and eighty-five were certified.

With all of the schools operating on the West Coast, that number of attendees was not anticipated. It graphically illustrated the need for Bane-Clene to conduct schools in other parts of the country. Later that year, another school was held in Las Vegas as well as one in Orlando, Florida. The success of these efforts resulted in our conducting regional schools throughout the United States.

Trucks pulled up to door in Las Vegas

XVII

We Tried Other Things, Too!

Scavenger Service

Yogi Berra has a favorite saying, "When you come to a fork in the road, take it!" As we look back on our career in the cleaning industry, it is easy to see all of the many forks in the road we have taken. At the time, however, it was not always clear what our path should be. Many business ventures did not work out, and some others were cut short before they had time to develop.

We went into the scavenger business in 1966. Sharp Ford was a large auto dealership on the south side of Indianapolis. Our janitorial contract called for the removal of trash as it did in many of our other commercial accounts. Tom Miles ran a scavenger service. We subcontracted the trash pickup to Tom, and he always did a great job for us, but one day when I was inspecting our work at Sharp Ford, I saw a large truck with a lift gate on the lot. It was for sale at a reasonable price, and I thought it would be perfect for hauling trash.

Billy and Donnie were not too excited about going into the scavenger business, but agreed that we buy the Ford truck. I notified Tom that we would no longer need his service. This was in the fall and the weather was nice. During the next three months, I had to hire six drivers because no one wanted to do this dirty job.

One cold, snowy Sunday morning in January, the driver didn't show up, and Billy and I jump-started the old Ford and began making the rounds of the truck terminals and car dealers. It was below zero, all of the barrels were frozen to the ground, and all of the trash was frozen inside them. What a day!

Monday morning, I called Tom Miles and said, *"Mea culpa."* He was very understanding, laughed a little and said he would take our account back again. He even was kind enough to buy that old Ford truck. Tom was a very nice man.

Were we ever glad to get out of that business!

Maid to Order

In 1967, I got the idea to start a maid service. We called it "Maid to Order" and specialized in cleaning apartments. We hired Harriett Ingle to manage the new service. She had worked with Elizabeth for Dr. Leeds. Vera Conn, who had been with us for several years, supervised the field operations.

Our office was located on East Tenth Street near a public school, and a little sign in the window attracted the attention of mothers walking their children to school. All of our maids were hired on a part-time basis, so this worked out very well.

Harriett and Vera would drop off two maids at each location with all of their tools and supplies and then pick them up later in the day. They would inspect the job and see that everything was in order before leaving.

It really worked rather well, but people didn't want to pay enough to make it profitable. I think we were just a little ahead of our time on this venture, since maid services have developed into a substantial industry.

We discontinued this service in 1969 in order to devote all of our resources and effort to the new carpet cleaning operation.

Carpet Sales

Something I always thought would be a good companion business to cleaning was the sale and installation of carpeting. In 1977, a local carpet retailer wanted us to buy his business and come to work for us. The idea had appeal and we strongly considered it.

One day the carpet retailer was sitting in my office, with his back to the door, discussing the transaction. I happened to look up, and there was Elizabeth shaking her head in the negative. She gave me the "out sign" that an umpire gives a base runner who is caught stealing.

I excused myself and went out to see what was the matter. She told me she had peeked in his truck and it was filthy. "Don't do it," she said. And we didn't.

The Big One

One day Sol Petruzzi asked me to come down and have lunch with him at Ayres. He asked if we would be interested in taking over the carpet department in Ayres' twelve stores as well as the warehouse workroom operation. Being flattered and cautious all at the same time, I said I'd get back to him and went about asking friends and acquaintances about the wisdom of taking on such a vast operation.

The first person I asked was Gene Haas, who had just retired as the head carpet buyer for Ayres. Gene said he didn't believe it would be a good idea. I called Gury Poletajev, at Lees Carpets, and he said the same thing. Howard Olansky of *Installation and Cleaning Specialist* magazine told me he thought it would be a mistake. All three gave me good advice and we took it.

Not long after that, Ayres closed the warehouse and did away with carpet sales for a few years. We don't know how the store would have proceeded if we had the carpet department, but we were very relieved that we had not taken on that obligation.

Seattle Opportunity?

Bob Grate had retired after twenty years at Lazarus in Columbus, Ohio. I met him when he came to our convention in 1974. Bob had been in charge of Lazarus' carpet workrooms in Columbus. He came to Indianapolis with his wife and joined Bane-Clene in February of 1981. Bob was a delightful man and had been brought up in the old-fashioned department store environment. He was truly customer oriented.

He had many friends in the business and was invaluable to our relationship with the department store industry. Later that year, Charles Brown called Bob to ask about setting up a carpet, upholstery and drapery cleaning department in Frederick & Nelson, a department store in Seattle, Washington.

Mr. Brown had been with Lazarus for many years and was the new president of the Seattle store. He remembered how involved Bob was in establishing carpet cleaning at Lazarus. Since Frederick & Nelson did not have such an operation, he wanted us to help him set one up.

We were not especially excited about managing a business in Seattle, but Bob and I flew there to meet with Mr. Brown. We convinced him that a licensed department would be a better way to do it and said we had a local operator who might be interested.

That evening we met with Dan Paulsen and his wife for dinner and proposed the arrangement. They were quick to say that they would not commit to the expansion that would be necessary to such an operation. Based on our St. Petersburg experience, we believed they would be running a five-truck business within three years. It apparently frightened them, and they declined to get involved.

In view of the way the department store business went during the next ten years, I think Dan did the right thing. But at the time, I was sure he was wrong.

Financing Equipment Sales

Early in our equipment sales business we discovered the need for easily available financing. Associates Finance was approached, along with several other national financial companies, and all of them turned us down. The CIT Group/Industrial Financing was the first to recognize our potential and financed several hundred of our machines to operators in all parts of the nation.

It seemed so easy that we decided to finance our own equipment as an investment. We hired Jim Allen, who managed a local CIT office, to head up our new branch. The situation reminded us of how Oliver Hardy used to say to Stan Laurel, "This is another fine mess you've gotten us into!"

The first unit we financed was to Bob Morgan in Dayton, Ohio. He never made the first payment. I remember my sinking feeling one day when I was passing Dayton, stopped at a phone booth along Interstate 70, and got a disconnect notice on his phone. We found out quickly that we knew absolutely nothing about the finance business and that Jim Allen knew even less than we did. CIT was probably glad to get rid of him.

After fifteen sales, we opted out of the financial world and began doing business with established financial institutions again.

The Window Cleaning Experience

Remember that old cliche, "I don't do windows"? One reason I wanted out of the janitorial business so badly was that part of our duties involved washing windows, and for me there are far more bad memories than good ones about window cleaning.

I remember our very first day in the cleaning business. It was below zero that February 4th, and I put window washer fluid in the water so it wouldn't freeze. It froze, anyway. We literally had to scrape the ice off the plate glass window at Dr. Leeds' office.

A High Ol' Time

As the company grew, we employed professional window cleaners who could do belt work, which entailed swinging from ledge to ledge with a safety belt that hooked to rings beside the windows. Professional cleaners also do scaffold drops on high-rise buildings. Jimmy Roberts was a great window cleaner. He was on top of the Union Federal Building one day when he called me to say his help had not shown up. So, I offered to assist him.

He said we would use "lookouts" for the drop. He was referring to four-by-fours that were eight feet in length. He laid these over the parapet of the building so they extended about two feet, and then put a couple of sandbags on the long end where the lookouts met the roof. It works through leverage, and I could understand how it was supposed to work.

Ropes from the ends of the scaffold were attached to the two-foot stubs that extended out over the side of the building. Then we gently lifted the stage itself over the edge. Jimmy climbed out on it and motioned for me to get on with him. I remember saying, "Are you serious? You don't expect me to climb onto that thing with you!" He was, and I did, but I don't think I've ever been so apprehensive about anything as I was when I looked down fourteen stories of glass wall to the sidewalk below.

Jimmy was a daredevil type and would take on any job. He even climbed into the cupolas at the Chrysler Corporation's electrical plant to clean a combination of lacquer and grease from the innards of the giant exhaust fans. What a terrible job! But, his downfall came on a simple little job that had him just four feet off the ground. He fell and was laid up for months while he recuperated.

Higher than a Kite

Another window cleaning experience comes to mind that definitely had a bearing on my wanting out of that business. Louie Allen was a great window cleaner. Watching him work was like watching a conductor direct a symphony. He was the epitome of grace in motion. Every move was orchestrated and none of his fluid motions were wasted. He was a master at his trade.

But Louie had this one little hang up. On payday he would get drunk and steal a car. He did this not once, but several times. His most notorious escapade occurred one Friday evening when he stole a car from the used car lot next to our office on Tenth Street and drove it to Pecos, Texas, where he was arrested.

The next time I heard from him, he was serving a six-year term in Huntsville prison and was filled with remorse. During the next two years he wrote to me every week extolling his new-found virtue and proclaiming his complete rehabilitation. Finally, I weakened and worked for more than a year with a local parole officer to arrange his release from prison in Texas. We sent an airline ticket, an advance on his first paycheck and waited for him to come back to Indianapolis.

He couldn't wait to get back to work. He was so thrilled to get out of prison and was so rehabilitated that it took nearly a month before he got drunk, stole our company truck and drove it to Dayton, Ohio, where he was arrested. Since he was on parole, the Dayton police contacted his parole officer in Indianapolis, who called me to ask what he should do about Louie. I said, "Keep him!"

That experience ended our social work and our window cleaning operation.

Jack of All Trades?

Every one of these less-than-successful experiences has taught us a lesson. We learned to stay with what we do best and to specialize. Concentrating on carpet, furniture and drapery cleaning services and becoming the very best in our profession has had a profound affect on our success.

In the years I have been in the industry, I have observed many people in the carpet cleaning business who fail, simply because they have diluted their efforts with diversification into areas in which they had no experience or knowledge, rather than concentrating on what they do best.

Those who have succeeded with diversification are those who have done so with adequate financing, competent advisors and a strong measure of determination. Most notable in these areas are dry cleaners and carpet retailers, to whom diversification into cleaning was a natural transition.

XVIII

Our Colleagues in the Industry

Competitors in the Supply Business

Jack Bates, the founder of Stanley Steemer, came to see us in 1973. He and his wife took Elizabeth and me to dinner and asked that we consider becoming partners in his new franchise venture.

I declined because of my fundamental feelings about franchising. I would not have made a good partner, but I was extremely flattered by his offer. Jack and his family have done extremely well, and Stanley Steemer is a major player in the service industry. Jack passed away in October of 1995.

Before Ralph Bloss owned Steamway, he called me once in awhile after we met in 1973 at the trade show in Cleveland. He asked me to become a distributor for Steamway products and said he admired the way my family worked together.

Ralph used to talk about his hope that his own sons would join him in business when they came of age. It eventually came to pass.

A Little Too Outspoken?

Perhaps the main reason we publish our own trade magazine is that I have always been a little too outspoken for most editors. But, I can say whatever I want in *The Cleaning Digest* without fear of reprisal by advertisers, because there are none.

I have written some articles for other trade publications over the years. In my estimation, the most encompassing have been for *Floor Focus* magazine. Frank O'Neill, the editor, had asked me to describe what I believed would be the future of the maintenance industry. This piece was published in December of 1994. In December of 1995 I wrote about the effect that declining carpet sales might have on the cleaning profession.

Dave Foster, producer of a radio program called "Floor Radio," calls occasionally to interview me on the air. Dave always tells me to say what I think and not to worry about what others think. The station in Dalton, Georgia, has a following of people in the carpet industry. I always consider it a big compliment when Dave calls me.

John Downey of *Cleanfax* magazine got me involved in a "Great Debate" in his publication. My opponent was Doyle Bloss of Steamway. Both of us offered our opinions on the temperature of the water used in the cleaning process and then rebutted the other's position. It was a colossal waste of time and ink since I believe that readers' opinions are not changed by these articles. They are only reinforced.

John has since published a very flattering piece about me in his magazine, which I really appreciated.

The Preacher

During many of my presentations, I recite "The Serenity Prayer." I believe it is the most concise advice for understanding the phenomenon we call "change." Change affects everyone and every business on a daily basis.

Chapter Eighteen

Lord, grant me the serenity to accept the things
I cannot change,
The courage to change the things that I can,
And the wisdom to know the difference.

The last line of that beautiful little prayer spells the difference between success and failure. I have always felt that accepting change and adapting to it is tantamount to survival. Knowing what we can and cannot change is one of the keys to success in business.

I lecture in my class at Bane-Clene Institute about change and use a comparison between business and religion in my presentation. There are religions that are thousands of years old, yet the life of the average business in the United States is only about eight years. I believe this is because business does not accept and adapt to changing times as do the various religions that have survived for centuries.

Editor Ann Hughes referred to my "evangelistic fervor." Kevin Finch, a consumer advocate for WTHR-TV in Indianapolis, called me "a crusader." It was probably for these reasons that a truck-mount equipment salesman tagged me the "Preacher of the Carpet Cleaning Industry." If you heard the name of the preacher to whom he compared me, you would know that this was not meant to be a compliment.

Another equipment salesman in Florida has called me the Glen Turner of the business. Mr. Turner, you may recall, was a promoter with a program called "Dare To Be Great." He got into trouble with the securities people and was charged with fraud for a pyramid scheme. Turner motivated people to sell his products and was considered a guru by many in the media. Some competitors in our business seized the opportunity, called me a guru and tried to establish a comparison by saying that people who come to our school are Bane-washed.

In spite of their insinuations, I believe these critics did my company more good than harm. Many people would call to tell me about salesmen who would call on them and spend most of their time explaining why they should not buy anything from Bill Bane. Most of them had not even heard of me until that time. Many who called to report these comparisons were actually quite miffed that people would talk about me like that.

I always said that I was glad they spelled my name right.

Threats

On more than one occasion I have been threatened either directly or by innuendo ... twice by members of the trade press.

Harold Arkoff of *Installation and Cleaning Specialist* told me that advertising the way we were would result in our being out of business within two years. We had cancelled our advertising in his magazine and put the money into advertising to carpet manufacturers. He called our effort "incestuous" and said that we couldn't expect to build our business by helping our own customers to build their businesses. That was in 1985.

In 1990, John Downey of *Cleanfax* magazine told me that if our company didn't support the IICUC certification program we would be "left in the dust," as John put it. I believe John was sincere in his encouragement to join that program. The fact was, however, that we had our own certification program and did not want to affiliate with anyone. This is still America, isn't it?

Ever since those ominous warnings, our referral network has continued to grow and gain even more support in the carpet industry.

Hate to Put You Out of Business!

In 1980, when Sears opened their carpet cleaning division in our town, Harry Stecker of RGM told me he really hated to open in Indianapolis. He said, "You're such nice people that I really hate to put you out of business." Sid Tuchman's general manager said approximately the same thing, and of course, I mentioned the comments of the vice-president of ChemLawn. Every time someone says they are going to put us out of business, we just get a little stronger.

The California Licensing Fiasco

Licensing of dry cleaning (furniture and draperies) in the State of California became a reality on June 1, 1984. A group of California cleaners got together and convinced the State that on-location cleaners should be licensed. Resulting legislation banned most equipment and put the licensing under the auspices of the State Board of Fabricare. The cleaners who had instigated passing of this law volunteered to test and license their competitors. It was a slick attempt to control competition.

The State Board of Fabricare was made up primarily of people who operated dry cleaning plants and were not sympathetic to on-location cleaners. As with any government overkill, a 228-page booklet with very small print came to cleaners, and just reading the regulations was more than most wanted to do.

Colleen Rhoades, a Bane-Clene operator from Nevada City, California, spearheaded a letter-writing campaign to eliminate the licensing law. Bob Quinn, Elizabeth's brother, lives in Pacific Grove, California. A two-term mayor of that city and active in California politics, Bob took an active role in lobbying against the ordinance. State legislators were informed of the ridiculous requirements and stipulations in the law.

Equipment had to be inspected, but there were no designated inspection sites.

The whole boondoggle ended quietly and mercifully when Governor George Deukmejian signed a bill on July 30, 1986. The bill had been introduced in the State Legislature by Assemblyman Wally Herger. They simply did not fund the Fabricare Board any longer, and this pulled the teeth of the whole sordid operation.

L to R, Dick and Edith Arnold, Elkhart, Indiana; Sandy and Scott Claypool, Mattoon, Illinois; and Bob Grate. Bob had come to Bane-Clene from Lazarus in Columbus, Ohio and was instrumental in this organizational meeting in June of 1980. A group of sixty Bane-Clene system owners formed the association which would become PCA.

PCA

The Professional Cleaners' Association (PCA) was organized so Bane-Clene systems owners could have a nationally-recognized association of their own without the pressure of sales-oriented groups, which are common in our business. After the great steam controversy was resolved, there was a void left by the dissolution of the Steam Carpet Cleaners' Association.

In June of 1980, sixty owners of our equipment came to Indianapolis to propose founding a new organization to be called the Bane-Clene Owners' Association. The name was changed to The Professional Cleaners' Association (PCA) to eliminate any possible sales affiliation or conflict of interest.

Lobbying has been a primary objective of this group. Fighting the California licensing law and changing labor laws to fit modern times were top priorities. A bill introduced by Indiana Congressman Andy Jacobs, Jr., did not make it out of committee because of a disappointing lack of support in the cleaning industry.

The House bill would have allowed technicians to be paid as outside salespeople and would have eliminated conflicts with national labor laws. Currently, truck employees are considered in a class with laundry workers, according to the letter of the law. Those laws were written when carpet cleaning was done in plants that were notorious for being sweat shops.

Educating consumer affairs agencies is high on the association's agenda. Regular mailings to consumer advocates and politicians makes the voice of the group heard. A few of those who have worked with PCA in consumer-related matters are Brea Walker, a Los Angeles, California, television anchor; Charlotte Sutton, a feature writer for the St. Petersburg, Florida, *Times*; Joe Ducey of Channel 8 in Tampa, Florida; Ken Amaro of Channel 12, Jacksonville, Florida; Rosanne Colletti of Channel 2 in New York City; and Kevin Finch, of Channel 13, Indianapolis, Indiana.

Today there are members of the PCA in all fifty states, Canada, Mexico, the Virgin Islands and the United Kingdom.

Other Associations

Training and certifying cleaning operators is not a new idea. Bane-Clene has had a training program since 1971 and a certification program since 1978. One of the early proponents of training and certification was Ed York. He organized the International Institute of Carpet and Upholstery Cleaners (IICUC). Ed controlled that organization until the other interests bought his stock.

In 1993, the IICUC was changed to IICRC (International Institute of Cleaning and Restoration Certification). Ironically, some of the players in the IICRC were involved in the California licensing fiasco.

The idea of IICUC certification was a good one, but the logistics of having salesmen conduct nonparochial schools was next to impossible. Hidden agendas surface during so-called training classes. Bane-Clene Institute has had success in schooling because there is no secret about the products involved in the school.

I have encouraged prominent people in the carpet industry to support the idea of eliminating "generic" schools and encouraging the manufacturers of equipment and chemicals to pay for their own educational programs.

Either the IICRC or CRI (Carpet and Rug Institute) could serve as an accrediting body to ensure that necessary curriculum was included in each school.

This would eliminate the subterfuge and would improve training programs by following a curriculum which would concern the products of that company. We have done this since the beginning, and it has been extremely successful.

Two other companies who offer good parochial schools are Von Schrader and Host (Racine Industries, Inc.)

ICRA

In 1993 an organization called Institute of Cleaning and Restoration Associations (ICRA) was formed. It was supposed to encompass all industry associations under one umbrella. I was invited to a meeting in Toledo, Ohio, and PCA was asked to be a part of ICRA. The organization was not accepted by the industry and was disbanded within a year.

The ICRA agenda has been transferred to the IICRC. In 1995, Bane-Clene was invited to sit on the certification board of the IICRC. Kevin Stark accepted the invitation to serve on the board.

SCT

The Society of Cleaning Technicians (SCT) was also organized by Ed York. One of the early associations of on-location cleaning firms, SCT was Ed's answer to the AIDS organization, which ignored the on-location segment of the industry. I organized the Steam Carpet Cleaners' Association (SCCA) in 1974, and Ed's group was already in business. I don't know what year he began, but we worked toward mutual goals in The Great Steam Controversy.

SCT had a publication called *Tips 'n Chat*, which was widely circulated in the industry. It was a good publication, and it's a shame it did not survive. York started several franchises and was always ahead of the times, but didn't seem to have the patience to stay with anything long enough for it to work. He sold the SCT to Sonny Bass in 1990, who, in turn, sold the association to Jeff Bishop. Bishop owns ProMaster, an equipment and chemical company. SCT's name was changed to ISCT (International Society of Cleaning Technicians) in 1992. Jeff has reportedly divested himself of ownership in ISCT. Joel and Kathy Reets, Sonny Bass, Walt Lipscomb, Ron Saunders, Ruth Travis, and Scott Warrington own the stock in ISCT.

ASCR

The Association of Specialists in Cleaning and Restoration (ASCR) was originally known as the Association of Interior Decor Specialists (AIDS). It was a shame that the disease came along and they had to change their name. ASCR is an association of the more affluent members of the cleaning and restoration profession. In recent years they have been most active in fire and water restoration.

In 1996 the ASCR celebrated their fiftieth anniversary.

Regional Associations

There are many regional and local associations in the industry. I have been critical of a few of these groups. If the management of a group includes salespeople, that's like letting a fox in the hen house. Some officers and directors are genuinely in the cleaning business, but others are indirectly involved in sales, and it's difficult to tell who the players are without a program.

Not all equipment and chemical salespeople who are involved in associations are bad guys. I have many friends in the industry who sell something. My objection has always been those who play at education and disguise themselves as teachers, while their real purpose is simply to sell products.

Hucksters

Murray Cremer put on a clinic everywhere he went.
He attended the 1976 SCCA convention in Indianapolis

In 1976, I organized a convention of the SCCA and invited competitors in the equipment and chemical business to exhibit. Murray Cremer, a pioneer of on-location drapery cleaning, was there with his KleenRite equipment and chemical line. Murray was one of the most exuberant individuals I have ever met and was a gentleman of the first order. He passed away in 1994.

I admired Murray Cremer and had several extensive conversations with him about the state of the industry. He told me that the SCCA meeting in 1976 was the best-run convention he had ever attended. His sales at that meeting were better than at any meeting at which he had exhibited. This was quite a compliment coming from a man who attended them all.

Murray was a salesman's salesman. In fact, he was so good that he sold Len Lepak, who ran our furniture cleaning plant at Ayres warehouse, a furniture cleaning tool. We make a very similar tool, but Lenny said, "I just couldn't say 'no' to him."

In one of our conversations, Murray expressed concern over some of the industry's associations. We saw eye-to-eye on this issue. For several years, he organized a traveling show called the "Innovators" in which he selected the participants. He told me this was the only way he could keep out the sleazy side of the industry.

Murray said he admired our Mini-Clinics and organized the "Innovators" to compete with them.

Dirty Tricks

There were sixteen exhibitors at the '76 SCCA convention at the Atkinson Hotel in Indianapolis. Not all of them were like Murray Cremer. He had warned me about some of the antics he had seen at other shows and about some of the deadbeats who traveled the circuit.

On the second day of the convention, someone deposited the entire contents of a sand urn, complete with cigarette butts, into the water tank of our display model. There is a good filtering system on our base unit, so whoever dumped the sand into our machine must have been terribly disappointed when we were able to complete our demonstration.

But the most vicious act came to light on the last day. When we drove our truck off the convention floor and down the ramp outside, there were no brakes. Someone had cut the hydraulic line. A little while later, the engine died. Someone had put sugar in the gas tank.

Three of the exhibitors never paid the association's registration fee. Two others beat the Atkinson Hotel out of money which the hotel management later tried to collect from me. One exhibitor was arrested on a "drunk and disorderly conduct" charge.

I felt sorry for the Atkinson and we went back and cleaned the brake fluid from the carpet in the convention hall, but I refused to pay them for the room, food and other charges that the exhibitors had left behind. Those were the responsibility of the hotel management to collect.

Fun Salesmen

Besides Murray Cremer, there were a few other class acts among our early competition. Herb Harpham of Certified, Bob Hughes of Chemspec, Mike Palmer of HydraMaster and Jim Rhoden of Prochem were high quality individuals who represented their companies with integrity.

One of the all-time fun guys in the business was Bob Langley, who sold HydraMaster equipment. I first met him at the New England Rug Cleaners' Convention on Cape Cod in 1976. Actually, Elizabeth met him first. She was walking past his outdoor booth while Bob was trying to attract a crowd for a demonstration.

No one was paying any attention to him, so when he asked if she would watch a demonstration, she said she would. Bob tried for fifteen minutes to start his machine. Failing, he asked her to come back later and asked if she was with anyone at the show. When she replied, "Bill Bane," she said Bob almost stepped on his lower lip.

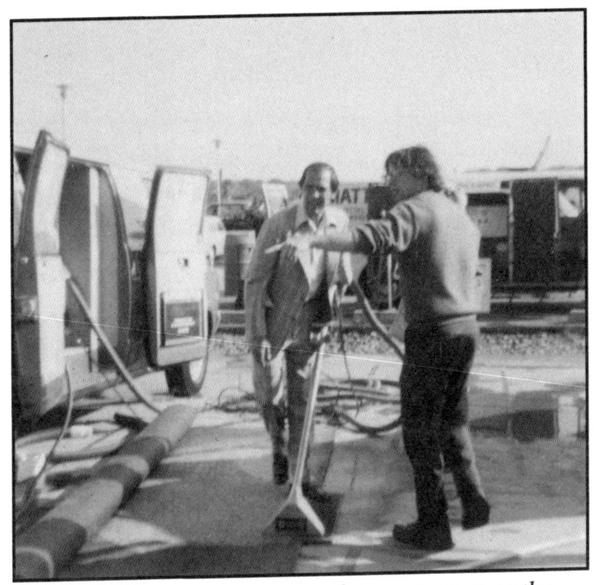

*Bob Langley demonstrates his equipment at the
NERCI meeting on Cape Cod in 1976.*

A year later, in Philadelphia, Bob was at the SCCA convention. He was scheduled to speak on the program about the advantages of truck-mounted operation. Gury Poletajev, Technical Director of Burlington Industries, was also on the program, and I had planned a practical joke on Gury. It was Halloween and the Marriott Hotel staff were all dressed in costumes. I asked them to parade in one door and out the other through the auditorium just after Gury's introduction.

The hotel staff didn't get it right, and fifteen of them came marching single file across the stage right after Bob Langley was introduced. He couldn't speak for a full minute and afterwards accused me of planning to disrupt his speech.

There you have the truth, Bob!

Con Artists

Over the years I have watched confidence men work our industry with skills that, if properly directed, could have made them wealthy. Instead, they make a few scores and move on when the majority of people begin to catch on.

In 1974 ads started appearing in trade magazines announcing a major breakthrough for the cleaning industry. "Remote control" carpet cleaning had arrived. The full page ad showed a little extraction machine making its way over a dirty carpet with no operator walking behind.

A few years later, ads in trade magazines touted "ultrasonic" carpet cleaning as a major breakthrough in technology. Plans were offered for building an ultrasonic machine. There is no way to know how many bogus sets of plans were sold to gullible carpet cleaners who were looking for a new and exciting way to make money.

Both remote control and ultrasonic carpet cleaning systems were merely come-ons to attract calls. Once a caller was on the line, the perpetrators would try to sell the unsuspecting caller something else. This was simply a variation of bait-and-switch advertising. Notice that they used popular terminology as titles to their scams.

Don't be surprised to see "microwave" carpet cleaning someday!

Fake Soil

An ad in an industry trade publication recently announced the introduction of synthetic soil. It costs "only" $56 a pound. Such a bargain! The purpose is to provide similarity and continuity of soiling carpet samples for testing. Seeing that ad for fake dirt made me think back to how we found the answers to the many problems relating to the cleaning business.

Whenever we wanted to try something new, we would bring a heavily soiled piece of carpet to our plant. These have always been easy to acquire from installation services. If we promised to pick up the old carpet at the job site, the installers really loved us for it. In fact, they would give us all the carpet we could ever dream of owning just for hauling it away.

By observing the kind of business or residence from which the carpet was taken and by asking a few questions, we were able to establish a pretty reliable history of the carpet and soiling conditions.

Once in place in our warehouse, masking off small areas and trying different techniques or products was simple. We did comparisons with most competitive equipment by using trade-in machines. By looking at the back of the carpet, we could find which ones had been over wet. By looking at the surface and using a magnifying glass, we could tell which ones were clean. By leaving the piece of carpet down in our warehouse we could check on how quickly it resoiled.

Chemicals were tested the same way. Some would say this is not very scientific, but we like the system because it's honest, simple and very effective. The major problem I have with artificial testing is that it is not done in the real world.

An eight-year-old carpet that has been exposed to children, pets, asphalt tracking, fume fading, and real feet grinding all of it into the fibers is an excellent candidate for testing cleaning products and methods. There is nothing artificial or contrived here.

Will I buy artificial dirt for $56 a pound? Hardly! P. T. Barnum said it best when he uttered that immortal statement, "There's a sucker born every minute."

XIX

The Ingredients Of A Winner

We've Been Blessed

People have been the key to our business success. Kevin Stark joined us in 1972 while he was working on his degree at Indiana University. A grade school friend of Billy's and Donnie's, he worked his way through school and then spent eight years in our service company before moving over to the supply side of the business. Kevin has worked in every department, and today is a vice-president of Bane-Clene Corporation.

Our first full-time telephone specialist, besides Elizabeth, was Doris Schubert, who joined the firm in 1972. Doris teaches a class on telephone procedures at Bane-Clene Institute. She has been a mainstay on the office staff, teaching new people how to give telephone quotes and handle routine office business.

Doris Schubert

The Quest For Productive People

I employed six different secretaries in 1975 while searching for someone to whom I could dictate a letter and have it come back to me in intelligible form. Some potential secretaries, who were interviewed through an agency, couldn't even type. We started buying "liquid paper" by the case.

Oka Negley

Elizabeth said I should have a secretary like Oka Negley, who could accurately type ninety words per minute and take shorthand as fast as I could speak. She was the secretary at Oaklandon Christian Church, and I said that if we recruited her there might be a clap of thunder from on high. We agreed that she probably would never leave the church, anyway.

Elizabeth was a member of Phi Delta Pi, a social sorority, and met Oka when she joined in 1953. Elizabeth mentioned our proposition at a sorority meeting and later took Oka to lunch to ask her to come with our company. She joined the firm in August of 1976. Today, she serves as my administrative assistant, supervises legal matters and coordinates all of the company's advertising programs.

Another Problem Solved

Bookkeeping was a nightmare for our young company. One employee stuffed invoices in her bottom desk drawer if she didn't have time to enter them when it was time to go home. We found a drawer full of old invoices which had not been posted when she left the company . Some of the other so-called bookkeepers had trouble counting to ten without using their fingers.

Denise Chilcote

In early 1977, a bright-eyed young lady came to us fresh out of school looking for a job. Her precise accounting practices and thorough, painstaking method of double-checking everything she did have made Denise Chilcote

Ron Baker

Marc Jones

Terry Harlan

Dan Willis

a major asset to our company. Denise has worked her way through the ranks of the accounting department and today is the Director of Corporate Accounting.

Ron Baker joined the company in 1978. Ron and Billy served in the military together. Ron and Marc Jones, also in our Sales Division, and Donnie played on a baseball team I managed in the late '60s. In fact, 1969 was a truly outstanding year. We won the State Baseball Championship, the Amazing Mets won the World Series, and that was the first year of our new carpet cleaning service business. Occasionally all of us reminisce about those feats.

Terry Harlan, who is responsible for the manufacture of our equipment, began his career with us in 1979. Terry was a skilled carpet installer when he joined our firm. He worked as a cleaning technician for six years before coming inside and working on the assembly of our equipment. Today he manages the entire production facility.

Our service company is managed by Dan Willis, who joined us in 1984. After five years as a cleaning technician, he was moved into the office and then promoted to the position of Manager of the Wm. F. Bane Company, which is a wholly-owned subsidiary of Bane-Clene Corporation.

Customer Friendly

Everyone at Bane-Clene has spent time in the cleaning business, even though some brought other expertise to the company. For example, when Joe Huser joined us, it was in an engineering capacity. While working as an engineer in the design and modification of our equipment, Joe got excited about the business, spent time on a cleaning truck and joined the sales staff. His engineering background lends a strong technical support aspect to his customer service duties.

Mike Perry joined the company as a technician, worked in that capacity for six years and then moved into customer service. This experience has been invaluable to Mike's clients. Rich Voyles brought extensive sales experience to the company. Nick Snyder majored in marketing in college and worked for an advertising agency before joining the company.

I would be remiss unless I mentioned those who have passed away. Vera Conn, Virginia Stump, Barbara Nye, and Bob White will always be remembered for their contributions to the success of our company.

Joe Huser

Mike Perry

Rich Voyles

Nick Snyder

Long-Term Commitment

Each member of our team has added significantly to the character of the company. The same openness we used with our family in the early years is practiced with our staff today. Any new ideas are brought to a monthly staff meeting, discussed, and consensus reached before any action is taken. Although many would say that we run our company by committee, I believe one of our strong points is the involvement of these loyal people in our decision-making process.

I believe one of the major problems in the business world today is the vast turnover in employees. It seems as if no one stays anywhere very long. The companies are the losers. By the time an employee learns something that will make a profit for the company, he or she is gone.

Our company has gone counter to the national trend of short-term employment and has attracted career-oriented people. Long-time business associates such as these have given us a terrific advantage over the competition.

Selling Our Business?

Rumors are constantly circulating in the industry that Bane-Clene is being sold or that the family has offered the company for sale. During the past ten years, we have had a dozen legitimate offers to buy the company. One offer from London, England, seemed the most serious. As of this time, we have no intention of selling Bane-Clene Corporation, and the family has never offered the company for sale.

Continuity

My youngest grandson, Brett, has talked about being the Chairman of the Board since he was two years old. One day

Brett and Pawpaw posed for this picture in 1985.

when Brett was about four, he was sitting at my office desk. Oka happened to come in. There he was with his little feet up on the desk. His short legs barely reached from the high-backed chair. He asked her, "Oka, will you be my secretary when I have this job?"

In 1988, when Brett was six, he attended our convention in Indianapolis. He walked up to Lucy Bean, a long-time friend and equipment owner from Maryland, and stuck out his hand. He introduced himself by saying, "I'm Brett Bane, future Chairman of the Board."

I have no intention of retiring, barring ill health, but when the time comes, Billy and Donnie are young and strong. Kevin Stark, Don Terry and Dan Willis manage the three

Matthew

Nancy

divisions of our company. But most important, we have several bright, young executives in the pipe line to carry on the management of our corporate interests.

On the family front, my grandson Matthew and his wife Nancy joined the firm after graduating from Indiana University in 1994. Matt worked in the warehouse during his time in high school and began his career after college as a cleaning technician. His computer skills are his forte and he will be of great value to the company in the future. Like everyone else in the company, he has learned the business from the bottom up.

Nancy majored in Mathematics and has become a valuable asset to our growing corporation.

Something I learned in managing a baseball team is that a winner has a strong bench. If someone gets hurt, another player must come off the bench and do as good or better a job than the one who could not play.

Several times in our business, people have left the company, and I'm pleased to say that someone else has always stepped in to do the job. Aside from missing the people who have left, our company doesn't suffer because of the talent waiting to get a chance to get into the game.

We have the strength of continuity.

XX

Value and Service

Customers

Customer loyalty is fleeting, at best. The many thousands of our loyal service customers are still with us because of two factors . . . service and value. The best service in the world will not survive unless there is the perception of value by the customer.

Perhaps it was my experience at Gaseteria or Elizabeth's love for the old-fashioned, high-quality department store, but something always drove us to putting the customer first in every instance.

But, this isn't enough. A company must be profitable to achieve growth and to stay in business to serve those customers. Donnie has a saying, "It's not how much money you make; it's what you do with your money after you make it that counts."

The Turning Point

In 1981, our carpet cleaning service company was in great shape, but things were not going well for our supply company, which had a greater potential because of the unlimited market area. The country was still in the throes of double-digit inflation and exorbitant interest rates. We had lost the big Sears equipment contract that had consumed a large amount of our production time and, as I mentioned earlier, there was a lingering degree of backlash among some of our regular customers for our having done business with Sears.

Elizabeth and I had not been on a legitimate vacation since 1969 and had planned to go to Hawaii in January. Billy and Donnie insisted that we go. While we were away, they had to borrow $100,000 at 22 percent interest (that was only two points above the prime rate) on our line of credit with the bank to meet payroll and payables.

When we returned from our vacation, the four of us planned a strategy for the balance of the year that would change our lives forever. We decided to get out of debt as soon as possible.

Donnie became our Chief Financial Officer and set about examining every facet of our business. Contracts with major suppliers were carefully reviewed, and we discontinued two long-standing relationships in our chemical business and in the steel fabrication of our equipment. We terminated our affiliation with the ad agency with which we had done business for more than six years, and we renegotiated our agreements with the department stores and closed down Bane-Clene of Florida. We also published our first product catalog.

The last piece of our strategy puzzle was put into place with the computerization of our company. Billy took on the responsibility of learning about computers and buying all of the necessary hardware and software. With accurate records, we were able to pinpoint weaknesses and correct them.

These six major moves in 1981 turned our supply business around. That loan from the bank with its exorbitant interest rate was the last one we had to negotiate. On the bright side, it was the trigger that set our turn around in motion.

Staying Put

We have stayed in the same neighborhood since the founding of our company. Since 1982 all property acquisitions and building projects have been accomplished without bank loans. We pay no interest to anyone; therefore, our costs are governed by those of raw material, overhead and labor. Without mortgage and interest costs, our company is extremely competitive in price, while the quality of our products and services has constantly been improved.

It would have been nice to relocate to a posh suburb, but we decided that our customers really don't care where we are located as long as we deliver a high-quality product and service to them at a reasonable price.

If I had to isolate a primary "secret of success," this would be it.

Blessed

As I look back on my life, especially the last thirty-five years, I can't help but feel grateful for what God has given me: a loving, hard-working family, loyal customers, great business associates and success beyond my wildest expectations.

On the day Elizabeth and I were married, I got a haircut and a professional shave for this very important event in my life. When I paid the barber, I broke my last $5.00 bill. When we walked down the aisle, I had $4.00 in my pocket and payday was two weeks away.

I only had a forty-eight hour pass, and if we hadn't received some cash for wedding presents, we couldn't have gone on our day and a half honeymoon. That's starting out just about as poor as a couple can get.

The '62 Rambler we had to sell.

When we started our business, we were in debt, barely keeping our heads above the financial water line. We had to sell our old station wagon when we began the carpet cleaning business in 1969. I remember driving Elizabeth to church in a service truck because it was our only transportation. All of us remember the times when there wasn't enough money left on payday for family members to be paid.

I don't believe any of us ever dreamed we would one day be out of debt, drive expensive automobiles, have beautiful homes, a winter retreat in Florida and all the amenities that wealthy people enjoy. I never thought I would be a member of a country club and play golf several times each week or that I could take a vacation whenever I wished.

In fact, I don't feel wealthy in a monetary sense. What I consider real wealth is my family's ability to work together, the pleasure of daily contact with business associates, our wonderful staff, and the opportunity to see and talk with customers.

Most of all, I'm grateful that God put me here in this land that offers the opportunity to do what we have done.

The lines of a popular song come to mind as a fitting close:

> *Now . . . the end is near.*
> *As I face the final curtain,*
> *My friends, I'll say it clear;*
> *I'll state my case, of which I'm certain.*
>
> *I've lived a life that's full,*
> *I've traveled each and every highway,*
> *But more, much more than this,*
> *WE did it THEIR way.*

The Bane family, l. to r., Donnie, Linda, Bill, Elizabeth, Nancy, Matthew, Lois, Billy and Brett

Epilogue

"Doing it THEIR way" is the only way to deal with customers. Take care of them, and monetary reward will follow. Telling the truth and having the integrity to correct mistakes will produce envoys of good will that no sales force or advertising program could muster.

We Did It Their Way is about the success of our family. I hope this book helps you, if only by understanding that success is really the joy of dealing with the daily activities and problems that make being in business so interesting.

While the ending of this book may sound as though it is all over for me, actually this time is the beginning of the next phase of my life and the future of my company. As we approach the new millennium, it is, without a doubt, the most exciting time that any of us who have lived in the Twentieth Century are likely to experience.

Plans are presently being formulated to double our plant size during the next five years and, as I mentioned in the last chapter, key players have been recruited and are in place to take up the challenge of managing the company into the coming century.

Nineteen ninety-seven will be a special year for me. February 4th is the thirty-fifth anniversary of the founding of our company, April 26th will be the fiftieth anniversary of my marriage to Elizabeth, and June 25th will be my seventieth birthday. That's a big year!

Even though we may never meet in person, by reading this book we have, in some small way, become friends.

Thank you.

Wm. F. Bane